On Message

On Message
Precision communication for the digital age

THEO THEOBALD

LONDON PHILADELPHIA NEW DELHI

Publisher's note

Every possible effort has been made to ensure that the information contained in this book is accurate at the time of going to press, and the publishers and author cannot accept responsibility for any errors or omissions, however caused. No responsibility for loss or damage occasioned to any person acting, or refraining from action, as a result of the material in this publication can be accepted by the editor, the publisher or the author.

First published in Great Britain and the United States in 2013 by Kogan Page Limited

120 Pentonville Road
London N1 9JN
United Kingdom
www.koganpage.com

1518 Walnut Street, Suite 1100
Philadelphia PA 19102
USA

4737/23 Ansari Road
Daryaganj
New Delhi 110002
India

ISBN 978 0 7494 6487 5
E-ISBN 978 0 7494 6488 2

British Library Cataloguing-in-Publication Data

A CIP record for this book is available from the British Library.

Library of Congress Cataloging-in-Publication Data

Theobald, Theo, 1957–
On Message : Precision Communication for the Digital Age / Theo Theobald. – 1st edition.
pages cm
ISBN 978-0-7494-6487-5 – ISBN 978-0-7494-6488-2 (ebook) 1. Business communication. 2. Online social networks. I. Title.
HF5718.T456 2013
659.14'4–dc23

2012026743

Typeset by Graphicraft Limited, Hong Kong
Printed and bound in India by Replika Press Pvt Ltd

Contents

Acknowledgements

Many thanks go to all the unseen contributors who have offered opinions and insight into this subject. In particular I am indebted to Roy Scotton, Lyn Rutter and Alistair Smith for their thoughts on story telling, to Christopher Hammond for his witty blog, Cary Cooper for advice and guidance and Laurence Marshall for his enduring support. As ever, I acknowledge the advice and mentoring of Ben, Nancy, Phil, Anne and Hazel whose continuing enthusiasm provided the impetus for this book.

Introduction

Noisy, isn't it?

In every way our world has become a louder place to live and it's going to get worse. It's noisier in the sense that we are bombarded by more and more messages every day; everyone seems to be crying out for our attention. From politicians who want our support, to competitors shouting about their latest achievements, retailers with their 'biggest ever sale' and opinion-formers testing our judgement on fashion, attitudes and trends. And where are we in all this, where is our voice? How do we make ourselves heard?

As individuals we don't have a limitless budget to mount a self-publicity campaign and in business we face competition from much bigger players, so we need to get smarter with our written communication: it needs to be incisive, relevant, engaging and delivered in a way that can't be ignored. The old adage of good communication remains true and content is still king, but in the digital age there is more. Now it is not simply what we say which matters, but also how we say it, when we say it and who we say it to.

Imagine someone receiving one of your messages, how do you want them to react? Perhaps with a knowing smile, a nod of approval, recognition of your insight or interest in your proposition. With really effective messaging we can galvanize people, get a reaction, encourage them to reply or take some action as a consequence. In business this can be an amazingly powerful tool for connecting us with a whole variety of stakeholders who take an interest in, or are affected by our activities. Whether we're selling a product, service, lifestyle or ideology the effect of powerful messaging is to garner loyalty, generate action and ultimately encourage evangelism on our part.

Although the world has become noisier, we do have one thing in our favour. Technology has become the great enabler in communication but it is not the hardware and software which has had the biggest effect, it is behaviour. Attitudes have changed and 'accessibility' is the new trend which has altered the way we think of personal and business relationships. Vague 'friend of a friend' relationships are hardening into real alliances between interested parties and with millions of online connections being made every day it is no longer thought of as pushy if we make the first approach. Suggesting a 'relationship of convenience' based on common ideals or goals is now the norm and we can begin the process of seeking out new partners to drive our businesses or personal ambitions forward.

In time we can build a community supported by a virtual intranet of our own creation. Whoever is within our circle will hear what we have to say and over time that circle will widen.

Setting ourselves this objective is the easy part, but exactly how in these days of information overload do we rise above the cacophony of din and stand out from the crowd?

The first thing to say is that 'less is more'. None of us has the time to read everything which comes our way. In fact a common analogy for consuming incoming communication is that it is 'like drinking from a fire hose'. As a hard-pressed executive once said, 'This pile here, this is the stuff I'm meant to read'. Enable your audience to get to the kernel of a message and they are much more likely to stay with you. Don't make it hard for them!

The logic of this is undeniable. If we are swamped with 'messaging' in the broadest sense, the only way to cut through the noise and get ourselves heard is by succinctly delivering powerful, memorable, consistent content.

In this context, what do we mean by consistency? To stay 'on message' means working out what the objectives are, devising a 'solution' and communicating this relentlessly in a meaningful, easy-to-grasp way. Business leaders have talked for many years about the 'elevator pitch', where we only have a few floors in the lift with the chief executive officer (CEO) to outline what we're setting out to achieve. When we're constructing our own messages, it is an excellent discipline to remember. Not only does it encourage brevity, but it also allows us the facility to deliver the same core content time and again, reinforcing our stance. This is important because often the differentiator in business is not so much what the message says, but what it says about us.

This leads us to a second fundamental tool: finding our voice. In this we have a head start as we are already unique, in thoughts, mannerisms, outlook and personality. The trick is to turn our personal idiosyncrasies into a way of 'speaking' to others through our written communication. In very many ways this process is much like branding, so we will examine in detail the skills of the marketers who have built international brands and sustained their value over many years. There are valuable lessons to be learned here, and seeing our messages as a key part of our personal branding will help to maintain the consistency we have talked about, as well as giving readers a shorthand method of judging who we are.

In daily life we come across 'clusters of language' which are in essence ways of speaking in different circumstances. There is advertising speak, political rhetoric and legal jargon, all of which are bound by profession. Beyond this we find sociological groupings; teenagers have their own language, Afro Caribbean communities often use 'patois', the aristocracy adopt 'the Queen's English'. What is common to all is that it is the individuals in these clusters who have found a voice which is theirs and theirs alone. It may draw heavily on the norms of their group, but each and every one is different. Developing and sustaining this voice makes our brand stand out from the crowd.

What follows here is a text which draws on the widest possible selection of sources, from political oratory, all the way through the science and art of marketing and promotion, along the road of technological and societal change, covering the ground of the advertising copywriter and encompassing the wonders of language through précis and precision. These are the strategies for getting our messages noticed by our 'targets'.

It is unthinkable that on this journey we wouldn't touch base with some of today's biggest names in social networking, but if Twitter gets frequent mentions or Facebook is used as a representation of the wider world of connectivity this is not an endorsement of them over their rivals. The digital communications marketplace is crowded already and is set to become even more so in the coming years, but it will take time to shake down; history teaches us that consolidation and competition will shape the future. However, as the technology constantly evolves, the principles of effective messaging will not change.

Whatever developments in hardware unfold, the trend will remain the same. There will be an increasing number of channels, content will become richer encompassing text, graphics, pictures and video. HD and 3D will make images brighter and more exciting, but the words we supplement them with will never lose their significance or ability to move or to motivate our audience.

In order to achieve this objective of effective messaging you will find a range of tools, techniques and tips to help you develop new skills:

- templates;
- simple formulae for better messaging;
- practise exercises;
- review techniques;
- step-by-step guides;
- ways of flexing your writing muscles;
- strategies to develop hard-hitting communication.

The simple truth is that boring messages are just boring. However, if what you say (through any channel) is vibrant, readable, interesting and unique you will always attract an audience and your messages will stick.

Use the practical exercises, plan your own communication strategy and develop a digital social networking presence that will rise above the noise.

Make your voice heard!

Section One
The digital landscape: context, competition and technology change

All the excitement of sitting down to write fabulous new copy which will catapult your business into the stratosphere is coming up soon, be patient! Firstly we need to get a real understanding of communication in the social media age. In this section we will take a look back at the journey so far, get a grip on what the new channels look like now and think about the challenges our businesses face in getting their voices heard. Before long we'll get down to the serious business of writing in an engaging way.

Chapter One
How did we get here?

Now is a great time to be thinking about our communication, because for a host of reasons our potential to make a real impact is greater than ever before. Part of this is to do with access to audiences in a way which would have cost a fortune in advertising spend only a few years ago. Today we can link to a niche segment who are actively interested in our offering and deliver real value through both our product and our messaging. What has brought this about? How was it exactly that we got to here?

We begin by taking a look at the recent evolution of messaging, which has catapulted us from a handful of hard-won connections with partners who were probably reticent at first, right through to hordes of potential new 'friends' both business and personal who simply can't wait to be linked to us. And it's not just the availability of like-minded people, but their (and our) *desire* to be better connected which is so significant. Online the reserve we all may have felt over new relationships has evaporated.

Where social networking began

Friends Reunited created an incredible buzz when it was launched and this hasn't died down; if anything, the excitement has increased.

The site was generally recognized to have been inspired by its United States (US) predecessor 'classmates.com'. Friends Reunited became a web presence which popularized the practise of linking up with former colleagues and associates. It began to point the way to the future.

Started in July 2000, the first signs of social networking soon became apparent. By the end of the year Friends Reunited had 3,000 users; at its peak in 2003 it was attracting 20,000 new members every day. Collectively we were beginning to discover that connectedness was no longer restricted to our address book or Rolodex. The realization began to dawn that we could now be linked with anyone, or everyone else in the world who had an internet connection. Once that number increased beyond those who had installed a desktop PC to encompass anyone with a web-enabled phone, the infrastructure was virtually complete.

As Myspace, Bebo and Facebook began to appear we soon discovered new features to enrich our social networking and the success of Friends Reunited began to wane. It still has significant numbers of members and traffic but many former users have 'been there, done that' and now moved on. Before we get carried away with this evolution there are some practical aspects of this 'founding father' to consider as a starting point for creating short messages.

An opportunity to engage

With any form of communication we tend to take a lead from what has gone before. Why do all radio commercials sound similar, how can it be that personal profiles on sites like Friends Reunited appear to be interchangeable? The reason is most of us start with little idea of how to really engage; instead we rely on what has gone before as a template for what we should write.

This is the sort of thing we might expect to find:

> Married with two kids aged 6 and 8. Living in Southwold, working as an accountant. Would love to hear from anyone who was in the class of '84.

It hardly grabs the attention and is made even less dynamic by it's similarity to so many other entries, it feels like a cut and paste solution. Instead, a better entry might be like this:

> Hi there class of '84! Was about to suggest we organize a reunion, but not sure how quickly I could lose 2 stone and grow my hair back.

I'm guessing most of you are now rocket scientists or movie stars, things haven't been quite so dynamic here but I eventually found someone who'd marry me and now have a couple of wonderful kids. You won't be surprised to know I became an accountant (remember, I was always top at maths!).

Get in touch if you remember the 'mysterious incident in the chemistry lab', the whereabouts of the Wilder Cup or how I got the nickname 'Giddy', in fact get in touch even if you don't!

How is this example different from the norm and what elements could we incorporate into our own messages as a result?

The first thing to note is that the opening puts the focus on the reader rather than the writer, drawing them into the rest of the message. The tone is chatty and witty (which of us hasn't noticed the signs of ageing?) and as well as being self-effacing it acknowledges a universal truth which the audience can feel connected to.

Finally, to take the reader 'right back there' it mentions some of the things that only 'the class of 84' would know about, adding a sense of an exclusive club which they are members of. One final lesson is that the ages of the children are deliberately omitted. This has been done because most entries on Friends Reunited seldom get updated; people's children remain the same age year after year! Later we will see how the evolution of this kind of media has necessitated regular updates, but in the early days the static nature of messaging is what caused us to move on to more dynamic sites.

The evolution of social networking

Exercise 1.1: On the basis of these learning points, write your own version of a profile statement

When you have done this, ask yourself one simple question: 'Would I want to get in contact with this person?'

One of the facts of life when it comes to technology is that the pace of change is ever quickening. As in any business, if you want to build competitive advantage you have to keep moving forward. What features can you add to existing products which will make them more appealing to buyers? While we all stop and contemplate what they might be for our own enterprise, let's return to the subject of social networking, pioneered to a great degree by Friends Reunited.

Added value in their bit of the marketplace came about through a number of routes. Some of this was to do with bandwidth. Of course pictures could be added to a profile on the original site, but what was missing was that no one saw the point: why post a current picture so people could judge how much you'd aged?! In fact, beyond the fun of nostalgia, why look back at all?

Reunions which came about as a consequence of Friends Reunited tended to follow a pattern. People said 'it was great to meet up and talk about old times' but there was an end to it. For the vast majority it was a one-off, not something you'd want to do every week; in fact if we really had missed our old school friends so much, why hadn't we kept in touch in the interim?

Fundamentally what Bebo, Facebook and others recognized is that the connections which could be made had limited value when steeped in the past. The future, if you'll pardon the paradox, was in the present. The important point to learn here is the technology was simply an enabler, nothing more. If you really want to understand how people will behave and the things which will motivate them, you have to think through the sociological implications of what is happening.

It's not just what's in our lives (like iPads and smartphones) but how we live our lives which really matters. The linking up of technological advancement and the human side of connections will always be critical to the development of communication channels. When the first phone directory was produced it was only a page long because up to that point a mere 90-odd people had phones. Individually we need first of all to become convinced, and secondly to have enough money to invest for a new technology to take off.

Naturally, there is a snowball effect as the more individuals who come on stream, the greater the usefulness of the tool; it becomes self-fulfilling. Eventually, it is those technology-resistant laggards who get left behind as the rest of the world gets on with its texting, or tweeting, or whatever comes along next; they end up living on the outside, still not really 'getting it'.

So, following on from Friends Reunited, what was it which brought about a revolution in social networking? As described above it was a combination of the method becoming available (with the introduction of much more dynamic sites like Bebo) along with the existence of a hungry band of users and potential users who had discovered a 'new' way of communicating with each other. Perhaps the most appealing feature of the new sites was the facility to connect with people who we'd never met before, simply on the basis that we shared a friend, an interest or an outlook. In our everyday lives it would have taken a decade to seek out like-minded individuals who agreed with our opinions on politics or religion, art or music; online it is virtually instantaneous. But wait, this is only half of it; the expectation of user behaviour is we will dip in and out of whatever takes our fancy on any particular day. With close friends we might expect a greater level of personal interaction, but in the wider community no one thinks twice of a user who replies to an occasional post but is not fully engaged in every debate.

So the upshot of this is we can segment our relationships according to what suits us. I may join in on a thread about the damage we're doing to our planet, but not be motivated to comment on who has been thrown off the latest celebrity reality show. And the community is so wide and diverse that no one thinks any the less of me for this.

Why does this matter? In a business sense it gives us a vehicle for targeting our messages with a level of precision which has never been available before. The reason is that our audience or 'market segment' self-select on the basis of how interested they are in what we say; suddenly the significance of great short messaging takes a massive step up.

The small business which sells fishing tackle could spend a fortune advertising in different publications to try and reach the wide age range which might be attracted to shop there. What would happen instead if anglers opted in of their own volition? By driving the right messages towards them, they may choose to follow us.

What might turn them on to this? How about top tips on how to cast, the best bait per type of fishing, what the experts say, the anglers calendar, where to go fishing when?

Exercise 1.2 Off the top of my head!

Our first ideas are often the best. The list of topics for anglers above was composed with little knowledge of the sport; they are simply the obvious things which first hit you. Similarly, to begin the process of devising topics to cover, write down seven headlines for your own segment which would cover the type of things your prospective audience members would want to know.

Don't be restricted by your own knowledge (so you could include 'what the experts say' without yet knowing what that is); you can always do some research later. Instead this is an exercise in understanding the overall direction of your communication.

Coming of age

Social networking really began to gather momentum. Running along on parallel tracks were the newly invented technologies and the social freedom they brought about. People were saying 'look what you can do now!' and more of us jumped on the bandwagon. The speed of these new developments was part of the story, but so too was the 'relevance'.

One could argue when texting first came along that it was a novelty for kids. That's certainly how many older people viewed it at the time; who would have guessed how mainstream it would become? However, offer a technology which does something 'useful' to the right group and they will seize upon it.

Supporting our new ability to link in to just about anyone was the development of greater and greater bandwidth so that once our bonds were made we could send ever-richer content to each other, in the form of not only text, but also picture, audio and video. Take our anglers again. Let's say through social networking I have linked with a fisherman in Australia. Now instead of discussing our hobby via written messages, I can let him see through photographs

FIGURE 1 Exploiting the available media

Begin by writing your message, then think about how it can be supplemented.

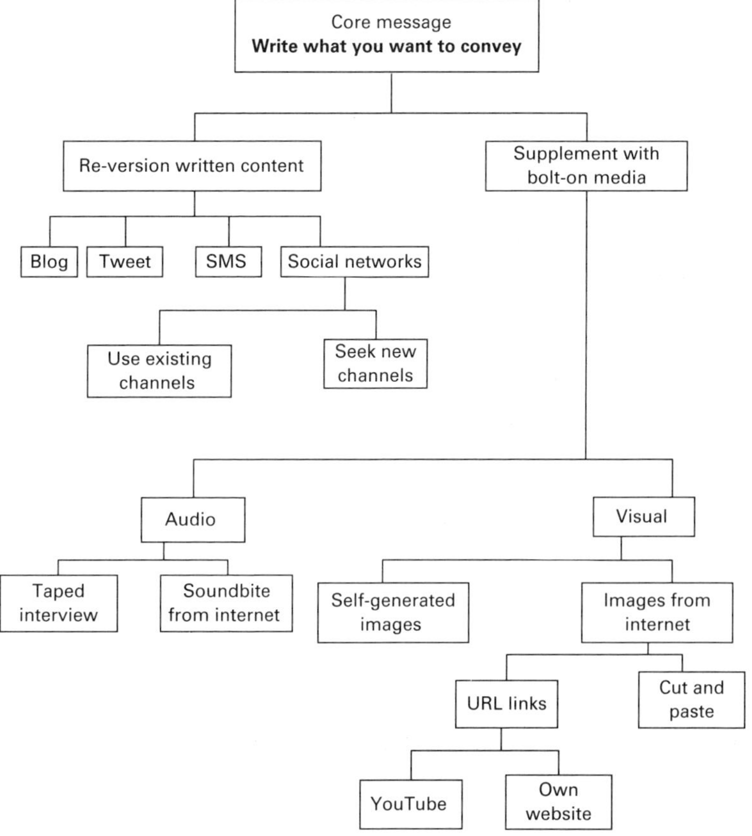

where I fish, I can even include video. Perhaps I use a particular technique: I can show him, literally, how I cast my line. If I am in business selling fishing gear, think how rich the content I can produce is; my messages can be written to really engage these enthusiasts and if I'm good enough at doing this they will come to trust me and what I sell.

Although this is where we are now, it is equally just the beginning. Competitive advantage, in social networking sites as elsewhere, is all to do with staying a step ahead, so we are guaranteed new developments to enrich our online experience.

Exploiting the available media

The onus is on us to utilize what is available today to the maximum of its capability, but also to keep an eye on the future. New developments are bound to come along, but as long as we build strong foundations into our digital communication strategy we will be able to adapt to whatever comes our way.

In short

- Linking up with old friends put new demands on our messaging skills.
- Engagement is built on relevance.
- Great messages will attract and keep a loyal audience.
- Take advantage of greater bandwidth: enhance messages with links to 'richer' content.

Tip

Keep moving forward. If you don't you'll lose relative market share to those who are.

Chapter Two
This is new media

'New' doesn't stay new very long any more, but so that we have a shared understanding of what the term means right now, this chapter concentrates on the latest developments in the communications spectrum, the vehicles we can use for our messages, alongside more traditional media.

This chapter offers an overview of channels which are currently available along with a critique on their usefulness. You will also find advice on how to set about the process of social networking in a measured way, which should bring better results for your future activity.

Blogs and tweets

Blogging takes its name from the amalgamation of 'web' and 'log' and refers to what amounts to an online diary of the user. There are no rules as to content or frequency of entry, but clearly there are ways of using the medium effectively and we shall examine some of them in a broad sense here. More detailed analysis of blogging comes later in Chapter 7.

Twitter took this concept and shrunk it down, so instead of being able to write a few paragraphs about a topic, the site restricts us to 140 characters (including punctuation) per message. Clearly this has had a number of implications, not least the need to encapsulate what we mean in an extremely tight and succinct way. This discipline in itself has altered the way people 'post' on Twitter, often linking to other areas of the internet which may contain articles, quotations, or photos and video. This means that in order to tempt users to 'click through', one of the great skills of the medium is similar to that of the headline writer, composing enticing copy which our audience will find irresistible.

Because Twitter's format allows for very quick updates, instantaneous reactions to what is going on around us, it has the added appeal of operating in real time. This can be massively powerful in business. Let's say we have a hardware store in a small town and have encouraged our customers to follow us on Twitter. As the first flakes of snow begin to fall, we can tweet to say, 'Snow! Looks pretty, feels slippery, clear the drive with a snow shovel, we're open until 8 p.m. tonight!'

A diary of tweets

What's at the core of your business? Do you provide a service or sell a range of goods? What are sales sensitive to? Is peak time the summer (if you retail cold drinks), or are there specific dates which cause a spike in demand (Valentine's Day for florists, Mothering Sunday for card shops). When are your customers looking for you? If you run a taxi service you could tweet early on a Friday evening when people are getting ready to go out.

Start to draw up a diary of sales activity and messages will naturally follow. Think too about those quieter times, what could you do to generate activity, perhaps a 'happy hour' or 10 per cent discount on a Monday?

To be a really effective communicator and to understand the power of short messaging in building community, reputation and status requires us to think carefully not just about the delivery channels which are available, but also about the human aspects of interaction with these tools. Both conventional blogs and Twitter have their critics as well as their advocates.

Just because the technology has allowed us to become 'enabled' doesn't mean we will all become avid users. Actor and comedian Stephen Fry is known for his omnipresent tweets; at the other end of the spectrum musician and former Oasis band member Noel Gallagher claims to have 'only just got a computer'. Both men live fully functioning lives, so is this enabling technology a 'must-have' or just a toy, a fad which will pass?

It's a fairly safe bet that Fry is right on this one. That is not to say that everyone who embarks on the blogging journey will see it through. There are those who have embraced the idea with vigour and become recognized as emerging voices which speak for the people. This is why they have attracted large numbers of loyal followers. However there are many more who have begun blogging with enthusiasm, only to see it wither and eventually slide from their agenda. For countless thousands of people the blog has become like the diary of our youth, begun with gusto on January 1st, but out of steam before Easter.

The lesson this teaches us about social media is that it takes time and effort. More than this, it demands consistency. Whoever is following you on whichever platform will pretty soon become disillusioned if consistency wavers. Updating your Facebook status once a week and tweeting on an occasional 'only when you feel like it' basis is no way to build loyalty. Communication via these methods is hard work, time-consuming and taxing if you are going to make a success of it, but ultimately it is worth it.

Critics of social networking

The volume of traffic across different networking platforms makes it hard at first to sort the wheat from the chaff. Along the way, this has damaged the profile of the new technologies, especially amongst those who have not yet engaged with them.

The argument goes that there is such a massive amount of babble that it is impossible to find anything of any use. For many of us, we are not bothered in the slightest if our friends have just made themselves a cup of tea; we're happier catching up with them in real life when we don't really need to hear the trivia of their existence.

As in all communities there are also voices who we disagree with, and this can further turn people away from the medium. But all of this is to deny the sheer power of social networking across blogs, specialist sites like Facebook and micro versions such as Twitter.

Blaming the technology is pointless; it is users who bring it into disrepute. So how exactly do we get better at social networking?

Networking basics

Setting up a blog or Twitter account is technically very easy and facilitated by the plethora of sites offering step-by-step instructions. However, it is not the technicalities which are the issue, it is the usage. So, here we cover some of the big mistakes people make when they begin social networking. It's good to know this at the start because we may only get one chance to make an impression.

This may seem rather fundamental, but the question to ask yourself before you start broadcasting to the world is, 'Why am I doing this?' If you are not sure, it's probably best to leave it for now, at least until you can come up with a good reason.

Focus

The single greatest mistake made by new users of social media is in failing to ask themselves the question above; their output and usage is unfocussed and tangential. Unless your audience is made up of unfocussed tangential users it won't be long before they give up on you.

What's the point?

Consider carefully what you want to get out of your online presence and use the statements below to prompt your thinking.

- to increase business contacts;
- as a way of keeping customers informed;
- in order to respond instantly to changes in the marketplace;
- to highlight special offers or promotions;
- as a loyalty builder;

- to be seen as an authority in a niche area;
- so that I can network with like-minded people (both business and social);
- as a marketing tool for self or organization;
- to increase personal profile;
- in order to become better informed.

It may well be the case that you want to achieve multiple objectives with your online presence and as a consequence have ticked a few of the prompts (plus maybe one or two of your own), but consider carefully how to set about this. It is much better to separate out your respective 'personalities', keeping business and social groups apart from each other.

Think of how you already do this in real life. Though you are the same person in the workplace and when out with friends it is usual to show different aspects of our personality to each set of people. As a rival to Facebook, Google+ already allows for separate 'circles' who you can feed specific content to. Many of today's entrepreneurs use auction sites like eBay to buy and sell a range of goods. There is nothing stopping us having multiple strands to this activity, so we might sell both *Star Wars* memorabilia and musical instruments. Keeping the audiences for both sales outlets separate is more likely to achieve success, as the number of potential customers who fall into both circles is likely to be limited. By the same token, if you tweet to say you are going to be attending the *Star Wars* convention, the music-only part of the audience will be bewildered by the lack of relevance to their specialist interest and will begin to 'tune you out'.

Creating communities

Find your voice

Linked to this idea of our multifaceted personalities is the notion that we may use a different way to address diverse groups within

FIGURE 2 Creating communities

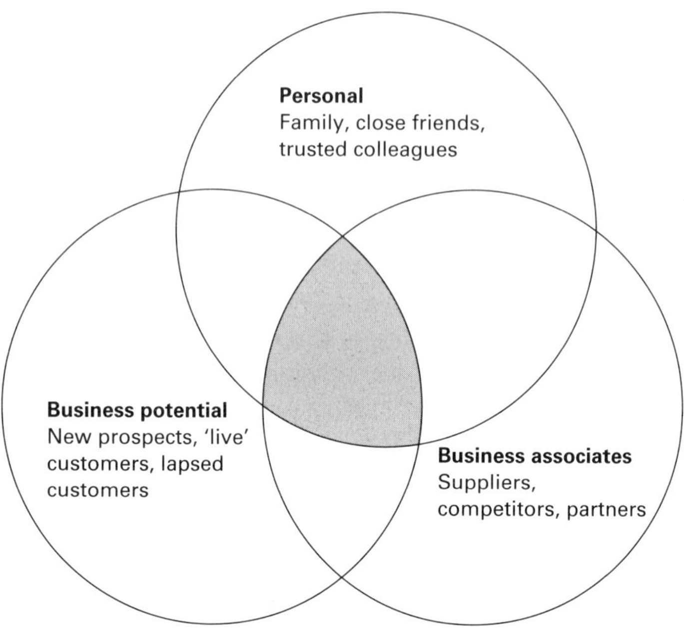

Consider carefully the message and tone of voice for each community.

Messages to all partners (in the shaded area) should be well thought through and relevant.

our lives. Informal language, use of slang or vernacular, even colourful language, may be regarded as socially acceptable in some circles; however it does not tend to translate well to the boardroom! The way we adapt to different social or business circumstances should be thought of in terms of our 'tone of voice'. These may be described and used in the following way.

The business voice

It sounds like this: professional, relevant, accurate, measured, serious, informed, knowledgeable, directive, confident.

We often use it to answer the phone or in new social situations before we have got the measure of the company we are in. It expresses itself as a kind of 'professional reserve', allowing us to feel our way through new relationships until we feel relaxed enough to ease back a little.

In meetings and in dialogue with clients the business voice is our default position.

The social voice

Relaxed, informal, jokey, laid-back, unrestricted, witty, irreverent, friendly, warm.

This is the voice we use when we are truly relaxed and being ourselves. As long as we use it appropriately it will help others warm to us and for this reason it often becomes the tone we adopt with business contacts we have come to know well. Be careful not to let this spill into over-familiarity: hierarchies exist in these relationships and we don't want to look as if we take them for granted.

In the past you may have instinctively lapsed into the right voice for the right occasion; most of us do because we have learned social norms and are bound by the barriers of what is acceptable. However, online this is something which requires forethought if it is to be delivered consistently and well. There are a whole range of people in our audience and they are engaging with us at different levels.

Before blogging or tweeting, ask yourself if you are being true to the aspect of your personality you want this particular audience to know. It's good to be conversational, but letting your language become too loose risks putting some people off.

Perhaps the most important advice of all when it comes to the voice you use it that it should be yours. It is desperately important that you show the world your individual personality; this is what makes you readable, unique and preferable to the competition. Hold that thought for now, we will return to this theme in more detail when we look at personal branding in Chapter 8.

Curb your ego

A cartoon appeared in a satirical magazine of a man sitting at a computer; above him was the phrase 'a typical blogger'. On the screen was written 'me, me, me, me...' until it filled the whole space. It's this kind of thing:

> Spent the morning getting wound up by the idiocy of others. Kids are playing me up again and wouldn't get up for school, then the traffic was a nightmare. When I popped in to get a newspaper I got stuck behind a woman who was paying for a chocolate bar with her debit card!!

Blogs and other social media shouldn't be used as a soap box to rant against the world; they are richer and deeper than that and are better served by those of us trying to create a dialogue, or provoke thought or action in our audience. We all share the daily frustrations, but what is the self-centred blog adding to that?

Of course it's personal, that is the point of a blog or tweet, but what we write should reflect our take on an issue in a way which others can relate to. Use this checklist to avoid becoming too me-centric:

- What is the issue I am writing about?
- Why have I chosen it? How does it impact on me?
- What can I do to encourage others to feel involved?
- How have I helped to inform other people (customers perhaps)?
- How are others feeling, on either side of the debate?
- Which feelings of mine will resonate with other people and, most importantly, why?
- How can I show my desire to expand my knowledge of the subject?

Establish your ground

Any opinion piece, whether in newsprint or on a website, should be just that: it should state one side of a debate. However, we risk coming across as bigoted if we don't take account of what the other side might be thinking. Try to keep in mind the quotation often attributed to Voltaire: 'I disapprove of what you say, but I will defend to the death your right to say it.'

A good way of appearing to be open-minded is to make a conscious effort to *be* more open-minded. Your blogging will probably improve as a result. Even when we are using our social media output as promotion for a business, we will have to back these messages with substance to make our audience take notice. So, some comment on work–life balance and the benefits of leisure might link to our fishing tackle shop without too much contrivance. When stating one side of a debate consider some of these phrases which would display a fair-minded and open attitude, without compromising your own point of view:

'I remain to be convinced that...'

'That's my view, you may see things differently'

'If you disagree, let me know'

'Can this state of affairs really be right...?'

There is nothing watered down about these statements; they simply illustrate your sense of fairness.

Another way of coming across as more open is to vary your posts so that not everything you do is focussed around your values and opinions. It is good sometimes to share what others may have said (re-tweeting is a great way of doing this) or to express your view on something which is already being hotly debated.

Be consistent

Whether you are McDonald's trying to build your brand or a politician with ambition, the rules of consistency apply equally. From a consumer point of view we are faced with so much choice that we really need some shortcuts to help us decide which burger to eat or which political party to vote for.

Many of these decisions are based on trust (I know what you're thinking when it comes to politicians!) and that faith is based on an unwavering promise. In the burger chain we don't expect the food to be different in every branch. Similarly, when we hear the politician speak we would be shocked if one espoused view was very right wing and the next much more to the left.

The audience you seek to attract are the same: they haven't the time or inclination to work out why one post is inconsistent with others; you must therefore make sure that each message reinforces the last, in terms of the voice used (see previous section) and the content.

This doesn't mean restricting our list of topics for discussion; instead it relies on an ability to 'talk the same language', whatever discourse we are involved in.

Keep consistent and you'll keep your followers.

Who will they hear?

Attempt to determine how you will sound by undertaking the following exercise. Think about a leader whose opinions you value; this could be a politician, business contact or community figure. Write a 50-word description of them and their communication style.

Repeat the exercise for a television personality; it could be an actor, journalist or comedian.

Finally, try to see yourself as others do and write another 50 words about you, from an outsider's perspective.

In future, try to live up to this description in a consistent way, so readers always get a sense of who you are.

Plan your activity

It really is pointless beginning a blog or twitter account with the attitude that it will come in useful when you think you have something to say. The initial burst of enthusiasm which normally accompanies the setting up of a new account means your frequency in the early days will be high, setting up an expectation which is virtually impossible to sustain.

The consistency we have just outlined with regard to voice and content is just as important when it comes to frequency of posting.

Writing a weekly blog is fine; just make sure you always deliver it at the same time so that your followers get used to expecting its arrival. Even a monthly update is sustainable as long as the entry is content-rich, enough to keep them on the edge of their seats until you post the next instalment.

Twitter is somewhat different because of its immediacy and small message size, so it will need much more frequent input.

Put the work in

Ideally, to build a real community, a proportion of your networking activity will involve two-way communication, proper interaction. If you continually fail to respond to someone who has taken the time to comment or reply to a post, they will soon lose interest.

In some ways the channels themselves govern expectations and most respondents won't anticipate an immediate reaction to something they interact with on your blog. We've mentioned the immediacy of Twitter which tends to set it apart. You really can't afford to leave it for a few days and expect nothing will happen.

Because of the sheer dynamism of the site you could be drawn to it 24 hours a day and many new users soon find a fascination which sees them hooked in the early stages. However, we do have real lives to be getting on with as well, so to strike a balance it is a good idea to set aside a portion of Twitter-time each day to keep the plates spinning.

This best practice of social networking is consistent with views about any other kind of communication; it takes time, effort and sensitivity to the audience. The debate still rages as to where things will settle down to. Having been provided with the ability to get connected with many new people, and with the rulebook rewritten on what constitutes a 'friend', there has been a 'gold rush' towards the creation of new online communities.

Don't be put off by the shifting sands of technology, or intimidated by the new trends in social networking which will inevitably come our way. Stick to the basics, follow the advice here and you will be prepared for the future, whatever it holds.

In short

- Social networking is here to stay. Its form may change with technology but the foundation stones are laid.
- Why are you blogging? If you can't answer this, take a step back.
- Keep your audiences separate: it simplifies the process and is more likely to deliver what they seek.
- Be consistent in terms of both voice and frequency.
- Set aside some regular social networking time.

Tip

Catch the slipstream of the movers and shakers and they'll find it impossible to pull away.

Chapter Three
Lessons from the past

We've looked at the evolution of web-enabled communication because that is where our written communication is now, but how did it get that way and, more to the point, is there anything we can learn from the past? This book advocates short messaging – it has become an essential part of today's communication – but the shortest message comes from the past.

Brevity is best

Oscar Wilde had just witnessed the publication of his latest work and, curious to find out whether the public had received it well, took the decision to ask the publisher about early sales figures. In these pre-email days, a telegram was despatched of such simplistic perfection that it was hard to top. The missive contained a single character, a question mark.

In response, the publisher matched the brilliance of the enquiry with a return telegram, stating that sales were indeed surpassing any expectation; it too contained only one character, an exclamation mark.

A very important lesson from this story is our understanding that both the relationship and the situation called for no more words to be used.

This means that author and publisher alike will have only one thing on their minds: 'I hope this sells!' So when the message from Wilde was received, there can have been no doubt about the subject of the enquiry.

Having interpreted this, an appropriate response to signal an excellent reception for the work was to express joy in the form of the exclamation mark. This also goes to show that in many instances there is much superfluous waffle in our communication and we need to remember that the padding adds nothing. Strip your content bare and it will jump from the page with much more energy.

Great communication is nothing new and there is much to learn from inspiring figures whose messages have hit home with maximum impact. The examples we shall look at are great speeches from the past. They started out as great pieces of writing and we can learn a lot about how to connect with an audience, how to move them, and the level of loyalty this can engender.

John F. Kennedy – 'Ich Bin Ein Berliner'

The context of Kennedy's famous speech is set against a backdrop of the post-World War II division of Germany, into East and West. Soviet occupation of the East was in sharp contrast to what was regarded as the 'freedom' of the West under the jurisdiction of the British, French and Americans. This division was symbolized most powerfully in the city of Berlin, where in 1961 the East German authorities had begun construction of a 12 foot high wall, bisecting the city, which eventually stretched 100 miles in length, preventing citizens fleeing to the West.

Kennedy's visit on June 26th 1963 was a turning point in signalling the US's commitment to supporting those in the West and championing their freedom from oppression.

The critical part of the speech, and the words which came to define it, was the use of the phrase 'Ich bin ein Berliner' (I am a Berliner) which was delivered to symbolize US attitudes towards the Soviets and show affinity with the people of West Berlin. It was a determined demonstration, designed to let those who had hitherto felt isolated and threatened in the west of the city understand that America would stand shoulder to shoulder with them in the name of freedom.

The set-up to the delivery of the iconic phrase was as follows:

> Two thousand years ago, the proudest boast was 'civis Romanus sum' [I am a Roman citizen]. Today, in the world of freedom, the proudest boast is 'Ich bin ein Berliner!'

In making the comparison with the Roman Empire, Kennedy flattered the people of West Berlin, but the real genius was in the proclamation designed to signal that the city represented freedom throughout the world, by claiming 'I am a Berliner'. The brevity and simplicity of the phrase was only part of its triumph. What sealed its place in oratory history was the translation into German, which reinforced the solidarity of the message. Kennedy's brilliance, stated above and repeated here, was that he showed *affinity*.

When we examine the complexities of this case study, it immediately becomes apparent that there is an intricate political backdrop to the speech. Kennedy and his speech-writers could have used an address that was several hours long in order to set up the pay-off, but by understanding what the audience wanted to hear, they were able to stay very much on message.

Kennedy, like other great communicators, shows us that often it is not just what is 'on the lines' which comes across to the audience, but also what is 'between the lines'. The signal about freedom which he sent in this address didn't need spelling out, and sometimes with our own writing we need to set up an idea and leave our audience to figure out the conclusion.

You could blog about your business, for example, using a 'customer story' told from their perspective and outlining what is great about your service. You don't then necessarily need a call to action imploring your audience to contact you; if they are convinced by the testimonial they will get in touch anyway.

There is an interesting lesson about language in the Kennedy speech. We have noted that a powerful addition was the translation of the key phrase into the native German of the audience, but why is that?

The significance is the attempt at *empathy* through speaking in someone else's tongue. Not only does it flatter them, but it also shows our willingness to extend an olive branch, a hand of friendship. We can view this in a literal sense by making an effort to match the language to the nation, but it is the underlying lesson which is more important. To get them to listen more intently, we need to talk like they talk. Whether it's the language of the street, business-speak or Swahili, the same lessons apply: match up, and you'll step up in your effectiveness.

Winston Churchill – 'Never was so much owed by so many to so few'

During World War II a beleaguered Britain was in danger of occupation by Nazi Germany. Prime Minister Winston Churchill, recognized as one of the finest leaders there has been, used a speech in the House of Commons on August 20th 1940 to inspire his people, whilst giving thanks to the 'few', a small band of fighter pilots who, against overwhelming odds, defeated the Luftwaffe to win what became known as the Battle of Britain.

It is thought that Churchill was initially moved to come up with the iconic phrase 'Never in the field of human conflict was so much owed by so many to so few' following a visit to RAF Uxbridge, where he had witnessed at first hand the operations room of the Battle of Britain. This signals the need to stay aware of things which move us and try to find ways of capturing those thoughts and words to use later.

It is reported that Churchill was genuinely moved by the efforts of his young pilots, who risked life and limb time and again in the cause of defending the nation. It turns out that his instincts in delivering the speech were right, as for the first time the Nazi war machine had been blown off course by the bravery of the British pilots.

As with Kennedy's speech, what Churchill did was to appeal at an emotional level to his audience. The use of repetition of the word 'so' ('so much, so many, so few') served to emphasize the monumental achievement and reinforced in the minds of a grateful public that it was not the number of aircraft they were able to deploy, but the determination of those who flew them. Here is the essence of his message. Every time we sit down to write we should re-read our efforts and think, 'What is the essence here?'

This phrase also employs the 'rule of three'. Three is the magic number of speech making and there is much evidence of its power. It can also be employed to good effect when we are writing. Think of recent British political history, where Tony Blair is synonymous with 'education, education, education'. Build lists of three into your own messages and see the difference it makes.

An interesting construct of Churchill's most memorable speeches is this use of repetition, and his realization of its power not only stood him in good stead at the time but has since been utilized by politicians, business leaders and communicators the world over.

The very fact that phrases such as these can be remembered and quoted by a majority of the population, even generations later, is a testament to their power. In a sense they were the forerunner to what has since become known as the sound bite. Unbeknown to Churchill at the time, his phrase was to have an additional everlasting effect, in that the 'few' became shorthand for the pilots who fought that battle.

Speech making has the added advantage of interpretation by an audience: they can see and hear the orator, process the words which are being said, but also judge the output in the light of body language, tone of voice or the passion of the delivery. What this means to us as writers is that we need to work even harder to ensure our written words alone will convey all the emotion we want them to. In their heads, our audience should be able to hear our 'voice' with all its inflections of mood, wit, sincerity or integrity.

Steve Jobs – Stanford address 2005

The final example is more recent and takes us to Stanford University in June 2005 when Apple's Steve Jobs addressed an audience of graduating students.

In classic style he began with a 'rule of three':

> Today I want to tell you three stories from my life. That's it. No big deal. Just three stories. The first story is about connecting the dots.

Jobs outlined how by dropping out of college he had time to attend calligraphy classes which although 'useless' at the time resulted in the array of fonts we now take for granted on Macs and PCs. His speech went on:

> You can't connect the dots looking forward; you can only connect them looking backwards. So you have to trust that the dots will somehow connect in your future. You have to trust in something. Your gut, destiny, life, karma, whatever. This approach has never let me down, and it has made all the difference in my life.

The second story is about being sacked from Apple and how it made him hungrier than ever to succeed. Then Jobs went on...

> My third story is about death. No one wants to die. Even people who want to go to heaven don't want to die to get there. And yet death is the destination we all share. No one has ever escaped it. And that is as it should be, because death is very likely the single best invention of life. It is life's change agent. It clears out the old to make way for the new. Right now the new is you, but some day not too long from now, you will gradually become the old and be cleared away. Sorry to be so dramatic, but it is quite true.
>
> Your time is limited, so don't waste it living someone else's life. Don't be trapped by dogma, which is living with the results of other people's thinking. Don't let the noise of others' opinions drown out your own inner voice and, most important, have the courage to follow your heart and intuition. They somehow already know what you truly want to become. Everything else is secondary.

The untimely death from cancer of Steve Jobs makes this speech all the more poignant in retrospect, but even at the time it contained critical elements of messaging which made it astoundingly powerful.

Jobs had achieved much success by this time, so he was able to share, in looking back, what it was that made him so. He said things which were new to the audience and counterintuitive to their belief system as graduates. He'd dropped out of college, followed his own path, done the things he loved and carried on regardless even when others criticized his approach.

To develop integrity we need to underpin our messages with beliefs and to get noticed we need to say something different.

This isn't as difficult as it may sound, for each of us *is* different; we simply need to find ways of expressing our uniqueness.

Jobs finished his speech like this:

> When I was young, there was an amazing publication called the *Whole Earth Catalog*, which was one of the bibles of my generation. It was created by a fellow named Stewart Brand not far from here in Menlo Park, and he brought it to life with his poetic touch. This was in the late 1960s, before personal computers and desktop publishing, so it was all made with typewriters, scissors and Polaroid cameras. It was sort of like Google in paperback form, 35 years before Google came along: it was idealistic, and overflowing with neat tools and great notions.
>
> Stewart and his team put out several issues of the *Whole Earth Catalog*, and then, when it had run its course, they put out a final issue. It was the mid-1970s, and I was your age. On the back cover of their final issue was a photograph of an early morning country road, the kind you might find yourself hitchhiking on if you were so adventurous. Beneath it were the words 'Stay hungry. Stay foolish'. It was their farewell message as they signed off. Stay hungry. Stay foolish. And I have always wished that for myself. And now, as you graduate to begin anew, I wish that for you. Stay hungry. Stay foolish.

For all the emotion and inspiration in Jobs's speech, it is his sign-off which can maybe teach us most. Keep in tune with the way your audience speaks, make it short and give it an edge. What could fulfil that brief better than 'stay hungry, stay foolish'?

Nine key lessons from great orators

1. Understand your audience, not just who they are, but how they feel, deep inside. Then show affinity (you don't have to have lived their life to relate to their life).
2. Think about underlying messages (the 'between the lines' things). What are you trying to convey? (Without spelling the whole thing out!)
3. Find a common 'language' (match up). One you find easy to speak and they will not only understand, but also relate to.
4. Notice the everyday things which move your emotions, whether happy, sad, angry or exasperated. Note them down and use this to drive more emotive content.

5. Repetition is powerful, powerful, powerful.
6. Re-create your voice in their heads by writing 'naturalistically' (that is, how you speak).
7. Dare to be different and show your personality and beliefs. Just make sure they are in line with what you message about.
8. If it suits you to do so, swim the opposite way to the mob, not just for the sake of it, but because of something you feel strongly about. You won't risk upsetting people if you can support your stance.
9. A powerful, tight sign-off to a message makes it stick in their mind, especially if it sums up the ethos of everything else you have said.

The point of looking at some of the icons of our age and the famous speeches they made is to inspire us. They are the forefathers of effective messaging for all the right reasons. They were memorable, emotive, in tune with the audience, short and relevant. If we were to apply that template to our own output it would make us more powerful communicators.

In short

- Be yourself – think about who you are and convey that in every message.
- Repetition is good, it embeds messages (as we have already said!).
- Employ the rule of three.
- Rely on your emotions, let them fuel your logic.

Tip

There is a correlation between experience and wisdom: think what you can learn from the past.

Chapter Four
What are we up against?

Recognizing the need to make our messages more effective, so we can cut through the noise and have our voice heard, is not a bad place to begin. It is also useful to see how communication has evolved and look at some of the shapers and influencers of that (as we did in the last chapter). But we don't live in a perfect world and if we are to maximize our success we need to think not only about the context and operating environment, but also about some of the barriers we might need to overcome along the way. That is what we will do in this chapter by anticipating and analysing these things and devising strategies to combat them.

The audience holds the power

The mistake many make, from politicians to business leaders and beyond, is that they think their agenda is the same as their audience's. For example, in the consumer energy market many millions are spent in trying to encourage us to switch from one supplier to another. Although this may have been an effective strategy ten years ago, we have become smarter consumers. Firstly, we have worked out that the gas and electricity are exactly the same wherever they come from (simply branded differently); and secondly, for many who have switched the process has been difficult and the net gain relatively short term. While suppliers may think our motivation is to save money, they have failed to take into account the hassle factor and lack of trust which have developed. Their messages (via expensive advertising agencies) may be beautifully crafted, but if they carry little credibility we are highly unlikely to respond.

When you fail to understand the lives, the feelings and the motivation of your audience, the message you are trying to put across will inevitably fall upon deaf ears. In a previous generation this lack of understanding may have simply upset a large number of individuals who had little influence. But now the landscape has shifted immeasurably. Today, with social networking, all these single disaffected people can join together and become a significant force with incredible speed.

No business likes to have a dissatisfied customer, but based on the adage that 'you can't please all the people all the time', it is bound to happen now and again. A letter of complaint could easily be dealt with, using tact and diplomacy, but if we upset a member of the online community today, the result can be much more difficult to contain.

Individuals are more empowered, so collective audiences who are better connected than ever before will inevitably share in this power. While on the one hand this can feel a little scary, it can also be turned to our benefit if we can gather around us a band of advocates or even evangelists who will spread the (positive) word on our behalf.

A fun manifestation of this has come in the form of 'flash mobs' who appear at a named venue by arrangement via social networks. They then 'perform' something like a dance and disperse just as quickly. It has little purpose other than sheer enjoyment, but it does establish the power of this type of media.

Opinions can be volatile

Perhaps what is even more of a difficulty is realizing how the pace of mood change can be accelerated. When we are bombarded by conflicting messages on a day-to-day basis it is harder than ever to form our opinions: first we may get swayed this way, then that.

In the world of manufacturing and retail short messaging has become an art form through the promotion of brands, aimed to positively influence the purchasing opinions of consumers. For years manufacturers have recognized the importance of branding as a way of sending a shortcut signal to consumers, a shortcut which says, 'You'll be fine if you trust this, you will get what you expect.'

Think of iconic brands from BMW to Unilever and onwards to Kellogg. All these companies have been successful in attributing qualities to their products which give us comfort when we buy them, so much so that they are often able to charge a premium over and above the competition. When we see a leading brand in a supermarket or car showroom, we are safe in the knowledge that millions of others before us have purchased it; it must be a safe bet. By the same token, brands say something about who we are: we become part of that 'elite' group who have made a similar purchasing decision. This is especially important where prestige products are concerned.

So, what is the link between consumer brands and our opinions? The truth is that we attach ourselves to 'communication brands' in exactly the same way, so when a broadcaster or newspaper we trust tells us their view, it can easily become our view. Eventually a 'relationship' builds whereby we know what they will 'think' about any issue, so when we see that opinion endorsed in newsprint or on screen, the circle of trust is complete.

Evidence of the strength of trust we put in communication brands comes from Simon Gulliford, a leading consultant and former group marketing and communications director at Barclays. Addressing an audience of BBC executives he said, 'I think of myself as a bright intelligent guy, so why is it that I *trust* the weather forecast on the BBC more than other stations? It's all coming from the same place.' Think how powerful your communications would become if, over time, your audience began to 'trust' you and your views over the competition. Because of the importance of brands as tools for expressing short messages, we will return to this topic later and examine it in more detail (see Chapter 8).

Opinion is dynamic for a lot of reasons, not least because how we feel about one issue is impacted upon by many others. An interesting example of this was shown in the falling sales of organic foods once economic conditions worsened. It seems we are happy to take an 'ethical' stance about where our food is sourced, and the welfare of animals which eventually end up on our table, until we have less money. Then such worthy considerations take second place to being able to pay the mortgage.

Knowing your audience is one thing, understanding the dynamics which might alter their opinion is another, and it is only by staying in touch with current thinking that we can keep our own messages relevant and accessible. Just when you thought you were getting a grip of what they were thinking, something comes along to change their minds. It's essential we keep up.

Information overload

On top of this we have to cope with a massive volume of information on a daily basis. As we said in our introduction, most of us have already lost the battle with the 'to-be-read' pile. This is even worse when we follow a dozen or more people on Twitter. Fail to check in every few minutes and you come back to hundreds of new tweets. It really can be very energy-sapping and the time we spend worrying about the incoming information we could be using to compose great outbound messages.

This does signal the necessity to keep our outward communication tight, though. If we do that, we can help our own audience digest what we have to say quickly. By giving them an even break, a chance to grasp the sense of what we're putting across, we may lessen the burden of their intake. Ultimately they may decide we are worth taking notice of, simply because we deliver the information they need in an easily consumable way.

Viewed like this, short messaging may be said to be an element of personal competitive advantage. As we seek to have our voices heard above the din, this could be the key to unlocking our audiences' hard-pressed attention span. It is increasingly likely as time goes by that the voices most likely to be heard are not necessarily the most intelligent or informed, but the ones which articulate their ideas most succinctly. There just isn't time for all the detail any more: it's about big ideas, delivered well; it's all about being pithy.

FIGURE 3 The narrowing hourglass

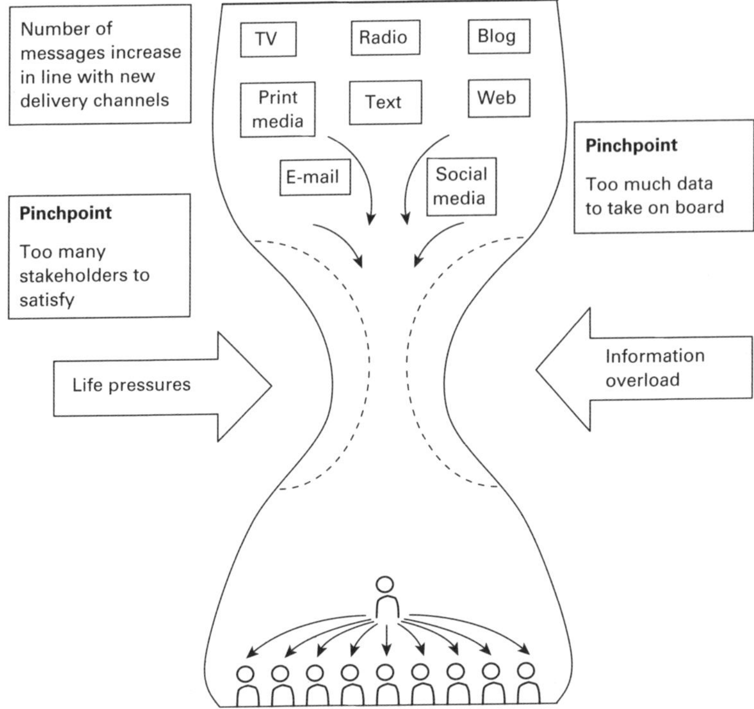

Audience becomes increasingly ambivalent and harder to impress

With the addition of each new wave of messages, added to increasing demands from work and home life, the audience becomes overwhelmed. Messages have to work harder and smarter to hit home.

The figure illustrates how an increase in the number of delivery channels and messages eventually leads to apathy and 'switch-off' among the audience. When we can no longer cope with all the information coming at us, we tune the majority of it out.

Technological malfunction

Technology is, in the main, fantastic. Without it we wouldn't be able to communicate nearly so effectively. That said, it has the capacity to be a villain as well as a hero. Being better connected through a variety of devices and channels (which seem to increase daily) is something we have fully embraced; it's really exciting. However, the paradox is this: the more ways we have of sending and receiving, the more we send and receive to the point where we simply can't cope with it any more (this is a major contributor to the overload just mentioned).

In very many ways we are just like our audience. All of us need to find a way to sort and filter the messages. As individuals, if we are trying to take back control of our own time, our own lives, we need to get better at assimilating what is coming in and editing what goes out. Our main focus has to be on getting our message out there; if we lose sight of that because of what is coming in, we lose a massive opportunity to influence.

So, for all these reasons, succinct communication has gone beyond being a luxury; it is one of the foundation stones of effective work, management and life.

In short

- Keep it tight. Short messages are full of impact.
- Who's listening? If you misunderstand the audience your message will fail.
- Keep in touch; opinions change, make sure you change with them.
- Messaging wisdom says, 'the bigger the haystack, the harder to find the needle'.
- Technology is a blunt instrument; it increases the number of messages but not the quality. We need to be smarter to cut through the noise.

Tip

Resilience is needed when demands are high and levels of control low. You can combat this if you have support. Go and find a new source soon.

Section Two
Guiding principles: stickiness and blogging

- all about stickiness;
- how to get stickier;
- thoughts about blogging.

Sticky messaging is the way forward, getting audiences not only to take notice of what we're saying, but also be drawn back to us as a trusted, reliable, insightful and possibly even witty source of news, information, comment and solution. Through this section we analyse what drives stickiness in messaging and consider this in the context of blogging, one of the foremost content-drivers for all modern businesses.

Chapter Five
All about stickiness

The term 'sticky messaging' is a product of the internet age. The idea is simple: how do we get people to stay with us and consume our communication, rather than drift off elsewhere? Although originally applied to websites, it is now just as relevant for any other type of messaging, especially the social media kind.

Let's examine the benefits and elements of stickiness so that we can begin to apply the important principles to our outbound messages and start the process of building a loyal, interested following in earnest.

How did the concept of stickiness evolve? When the first websites were developed they tended to be simply about giving information; no one thought much beyond this. The difficulty with this new medium was that few people had much idea how to use it effectively; many sites were just made up of pages cut and pasted from other forms of media. Long passages and blocks of text which needed scrolling through, not just vertically but left and right too, turned readers off. Pretty soon we were coming to realize that different reading habits were forming and both our content and design had to keep pace if we weren't going to bore our audience to death.

As understanding of menu-driven navigation increased, sites became easier to handle. We began as users to 'get into' the way of them and engage with where they attempted to take us. One of the first rules of this new game was 'managing expectation'. As well as having tighter, brighter copy, sites also need to be 'intuitive', which is to say users would get what they expected when they clicked on a link or navigation button.

Generally speaking, manufacturers of all kinds of technology products have tried hard to build this intuition in. There is much more emphasis on 'plug and play'. It seems we don't have the patience any more to read reams of instructions. The average teenager wouldn't be seen dead referring to the manual on their new smartphone, they just turn it on and learn 'on the job'. Their 'knowledge' is based on past experience of all kinds of devices; they are simply applying their intuition on this basis.

We are all like teenagers in this regard: we don't have the time or patience to hang about, and why should we? With such a vast choice of sites to browse, on any topic under the sun, why suffer?

These changes in attitude are important to bear in mind in relation to our messaging.

This isn't a manual for web design; most of us have already established our own sites, but there are some elements which can be applied in a wider sense to our messaging, to make it more appealing. Think about how these things could be applied across a range of platforms and remember they will be more relevant to things like blogs (which are limitless) than Twitter (restricted by the number of characters).

Web design elements which enhance our messaging

- Bullet points are better than blocked text.
- Reading times are slower from screen than hard copy: don't overload.
- Keep your sentences short.
- Occasionally the exclamation mark is appropriate, but don't overuse it!
- The more 'white space' there is, the greater the appeal of your text.
- Avoid clutter, whether it's 'offers', advertisements or peripheral text.
- Avoid garish colours unless you are trying to make a point with them.
- Check that text and background colours contrast enough to make reading easy.
- Don't use gimmicks.

The importance of short sentences is paramount and often it is simply a case of adding some punctuation and white space. A quick guide to better punctuation is outlined in Chapter 13. Have a look at the following two exercises and attempt to rewrite the text to make it punchier and more readable.

Exercise 5.1 Short sentencing

After you have made your own attempt at reformatting these long sentences, look at the sample answers at the end of this chapter.

1 'Body language is very much influenced by culture and it can be a significant cause of concern and uncertainty when dealing with people from differing ethnic backgrounds, especially if you are working with internationally diverse organizations which draw employees from many countries in the expectation that their partners, people like you, will be able to adapt quickly to these ever-changing needs, in order to avoid offending anyone.'

____

____

____

____

____

2 'Under certain circumstances management may be able to point to some aspects of organizational performance which are contrary to what is expected within the parameters of a modern business, especially one which has undergone extensive re-engineering in order to ensure it adheres to levels of propriety and corporate social responsibility of the highest order.'

____

____

____

____

____

____

How stickiness helps

No one would argue against stickiness in our messages as a good thing, but why, exactly? What benefits does it bring, aside from having our audience on the edge of their seats, waiting for our next post?

Two-way (social) listening

The best communication is achieved when both outputs and inputs are taken into consideration; it's not just what we say, but also what we hear.

Listening has always been regarded as an empathetic life skill and an essential tool of business, but that doesn't mean everyone has embraced it. Now, however, with the latent power of social media, it would only be a fool who would turn a deaf ear to what's out there in the marketplace.

We've already alluded to the challenge and the change brought about by the ease of linking up like-minded people. Instead of the lone voice in the wilderness, perhaps complaining about their phone company or broadband supplier, they can now begin a campaign of dissatisfaction. Before long this snowball effect can begin to cause big trouble for the corporation which failed to listen.

This example is perhaps a bit negative. Instead, think how beneficial the snowball effect can be if it's headed your way, full of new customers, people who might have heard about you through friends of friends. This is virtual word of mouth and it's fabulously powerful in building customer loyalty.

It is easy to see under this new set of rules how dangerous it would be not to listen to what is happening.

Keep up with dynamic evolution

There are excellent examples to reinforce what we have said about the power of social networking to garner mass support behind some kind of cause. The music charts are an example where online campaigns have frozen out pop pariahs (for the full story, search for 'Rage against the machine'). On a more serious note, the 'Arab Spring' which resulted in uprisings in many Middle Eastern countries was said to have been facilitated by social networking. No regime, no matter how oppressive, can control the news when it is developed by the people, for the people.

However, there are signs too that we are becoming resistant to and/or complacent about some of this activity. Online petitions presented to governments, which then take no action, are bound to discourage swathes of the population from taking part again; we may be headed for self-imposed inertia once more.

Track these developments in the media and keep looking for where the new openings occur.

Building an ever-ready audience

Everyone knows it is much easier to 'farm' existing contacts than 'hunt' for new ones, so if we can build up a loyal following we have the opportunity to deliver well-crafted, relevant messages to a group who are eager to hear from us, rather than reluctant to listen. This should create a virtuous circle if our messages are right, our 'snowball' will build and with stickiness we can keep adding to the size of our audience and developing their loyalty towards us.

As attention spans dwindle, a consequence of information overload and busy lives, our stickiness has to be built on ever-changing content: we need to continually refresh what we are saying. This is not like the relatively static nature of many websites; we need to offer enticing new messages to keep tempting people back. The next paragraph suggests some ways of maintaining excitement in our output.

Opinions, accord and answers

Being seen as a provider of these three things is a sure way to keep you 'front of mind' with your audience. Get inside the psyche of your target group by continually taking their temperature through feedback loops and you will have the opportunity to shape their thinking. It doesn't have to be about hard sell; sometimes the route to greater sales is a long, slow burn. Keep planting the seeds of information and eventually revenue will flow in.

What we're all seeking to do in the immediate term is to become a trusted source of information. Part of this will be about creating a brand for ourselves, which we will examine in more detail in Chapter 8.

Pulling the trigger

One of the golden rules of sales training is 'don't forget to ask for the sale!' So while we caution against being too pushy, remember there is a time to execute what is known as the 'call to action'.

'Pulling the trigger' is a metaphor for this; it is the essential purpose of what you are trying to communicate. Think, 'What do I want my audience to do with this information?'

Both of the following examples could be used in social networking circles, the first for a travel agency, the second for a local theatre, promoting a gig.

> Did you see the fantastic pictures of skiing in Aspen in this week's Sunday Bugle? ... go to www.buglepics/aspen.net to check them out, then book online with us before midnight for a 10% discount!

Or:

> Rave reviews for up-and-coming rock band Peng, check them out live at the Apollo on youtube. Last few tickets available on a first come, first served basis, go to www.lastpengtickets.com.

Don't make the audience do all the hard work by figuring out for themselves the purpose of your message, spell it out.

In practical terms this chapter makes a good case for stickiness. Knowing what it is and understanding the benefits is an important backdrop to developing those killer messages, but practical application is needed too.

In the next chapter, we'll examine the elements of stickiness that we can copy and use in our own communication, as well as showing how we can practise some of the techniques.

In short

- Stickiness is the holy grail of great short messaging.
- As the hardware gets easier to use, so the messages should get easier to consume.
- If the medium allows, build some basic design into your message, make it look right.
- Balance up not being too hard sell with knowing when to 'call to action'.

Tip

Keep it short!

Answers to exercise 5.1

1 Body language differs according to national culture. Be sensitive to this when dealing with people from different backgrounds. Global companies are very diverse and will expect you to be adaptable in your approach.

Explanation

There are a variety of answers which you could have written here and the importance of the new version is that it captures the essence of the original in a tighter way.

2 There may be aspects of operation which don't measure up to expected standards. This can happen even when attempts have been made to ensure ethical issues are addressed.

Explanation

This sentence is trickier to edit down because, like many, it is written in a much more flowery way than is necessary. The message, as ever, is 'keep it simple'.

Chapter Six
How to get stickier

Stickiness is built on two elements, emotion and practicality. We need to win our audience's hearts and minds if they are to stay with us. Here is a chance to consider these constructs of stickiness, not just in a theoretical sense, but also applied to your own communications output. Use the exercises as an opportunity to reflect on what you really want to say and have a go at outlining some messages which fit the criteria we will cover.

Let us deal with our logical, objective side first, what would be the stated needs of our audience if we were to ask about the kind of messages they would take notice of? Here are the practical building blocks:

Relevance

'What's in it for me?' When we're pressed for time this is a legitimate question to ask. Very quickly we need to be assured that the communication we are consuming resonates in some way, otherwise, we'll skip on elsewhere.

Message turn-ons

Here is a list of top topics which interest audiences

1 Something close to my heart (like my hobby, my family, my work).

2 New (the magic word of advertising!).

3 Information (what's happening in the world, especially my world).

4 Opinion (a different take on what is happening).

5 The word on the streets (what everyone else is talking about).

6 Personal (beauty, relationships, self-improvement).

7 Scandal (personal, business, political).

8 Difference (cultural oddities, lifestyles, outlooks).

If you want a great example of how mass media deliver personal relevance, buy a broadsheet newspaper at the weekend. Firstly, you will tend to go for one which broadly shares your political perspective, which is the first step in giving you content you will approve of. The next thing you notice are the many different sections related to more specialized interest. These might include sport, business, work, arts and entertainment, food or fashion. Interestingly, the format of each of these sections is matched to what is in them, so business pages look businesslike (perhaps not surprisingly) but food, entertainment or fashion may appear in a magazine format, reflecting their 'leisure' categorization.

We are drawn to our interests in a hierarchical way, maybe beginning with news (home and abroad) followed by 'what's happening in business', then a trawl through the sports pages. Each of us will take a different route, and that is the point, we become self-selecting according to interest and deliver our own relevance from the 'menu' on offer.

In our own businesses we can deliver relevance with a bit of reflective thought. If we sell ski gear, what do our adventurous outdoor customers do during the summer months? How else could we serve them? What products might they like? Think about your own business in terms of who the customers are, how they live, what they like. Imagine their life, imagine their lifestyle and you are half way to delivering relevant products, services and messages to them.

Step two is to replace your educated guesswork (above) with a bit of market testing. It's as simple as asking for feedback, or assessing the uptake of an offer (a sure way to measure if they liked it or not).

Combine what you originally thought with what you now know and you have a perfect template for relevance.

A final word of advice when it comes to relevance. Remember how dynamic it is, how quickly it can change. Kites aren't in big demand for most of the year, but on a windy day ...

What changes can happen in your line of business to do with weather, societal opinion, a news story, economic conditions or a host of other influences, things which might change demand or opinion, based on relevance? Look for real linkages, not spurious ones. The double glazing company that tweets 'it's a lovely sunny day, let more of it flood into your house with Crystalglass Glazing' is unlikely to get much response. However the same company could tweet following a news item on a new government report into energy efficiency, and link it to their product. Because this is real, valid and relevant it is much more likely to catch with an audience. Link in a special offer and this could turn a news story into sales.

This kind of responsiveness is extremely powerful. If you are able to quickly get a message out which comments on a highly topical issue, you will not only make a great connection with individuals, but may also attract a high degree of positive PR as the campaign or message is spread through word of mouth, online in a viral sense, or if lucky, via the mass media.

If we keep in mind the question all audiences ask – 'What's in it for me?' – then sense check our output (product, service, message) by saying to ourselves, 'What really is in it for them?' we won't go far wrong.

Universality

Of course there is great benefit in putting in the work to segment your audience in a way which improves the impact of your message. If we can isolate out the prospective purchasers of our goods or services we reduce the 'wastage' which often happens. With paid-for advertising this could be a serious issue because wastage costs money: effectively you're paying to get to people who would never consider buying from you. Most social media is free at the point of usage, so does it matter if we hit outside our target group? The truth is that we are likely to annoy these people, and as a fundamental principle of business this is to be avoided. Who knows if they may need our services in future, or be in a position to influence someone else? It's much better to try and keep all the people happy all of the time, or else it may come back to bite us.

Aside from customer segmentation there are some opportunities which have broader appeal, so spare a thought too for the mass market. To use universality and make it sticky there needs to be a high degree of cleverness applied. A banner headline which says, 'Aren't we all fed up with paying taxes?' will strike a chord with the majority of the population, but it's not clever enough to get a reaction. In order to sway people your way, you must make them sit up and think.

We probably all go through phases of wanting to be rich, or young, or thin or happy and achieve different levels of satisfaction with these aspects throughout our lives. We are wary too of those who promise us such things cheaply, usually believing, 'If it looks too good to be true, it probably is'. So the lesson is, don't make wild claims and don't overpromise.

You're less likely to get a response to 'Ten top tips to transform your life' than to 'Make this one simple change and in six weeks you'll notice the difference' (for an example of this look up 'Volvic Challenge' where you will find details of a campaign to get consumers to drink 1.5 litres of the bottled water a day, for 14 days). We all may have aspirations to make positive changes to our lives, but reality has to kick in too. The shift has to be incremental and achievable, it needs to fit with whatever else we are doing.

Observational comedy relies on picking out the seemingly mundane everyday things which happen to us all and highlighting them in an oblique way. This is universality in action and if you can hone your observational skills, notice people's common behaviours (for example guarding our personal number at the chip and pin machine, passing comment on the weather etcetera) you can begin to deliver messages which have relevance to a broader group.

Look out for themes which cut across age, gender and other segmentation boundaries and you will have taken a step towards making your messages universal. As a consequence, they will be more sticky.

No matter how carefully we hone down our individual market, some themes will play well across all of humanity. We all yearn for food, safety, love and inclusion, we're fearful of loneliness, rejection or not fitting in, and these themes underpin sticky messages time and again.

Solution

A lot of the time we're looking for answers, so messages which provide them are bound to be more appealing to us.

The difficulty with this area, whether online or offline, is that organizations shoe horn their product or service into a 'solution offer' which is not really answering a legitimate problem. Consumers are extremely savvy and if they don't see a need for something they won't buy it. It is estimated that around 80 per cent of new product launches fail, and the most common reason is that organizations really want us to want something, but we simply don't. Examples include mint-flavoured potato crisps and a new wine which came in a bottle with an integral handle in the glass!

This hits home to a fundamental principle of marketing and one which many non-marketers get confused with. In lots of organizations there is a belief that the marketing department is there to find ways of shifting product. If this sits anywhere, it might be more appropriate to make it the job of the sales department, although in many cases even this is questionable, because if you are offering something no one is really interested in, should you waste your sales resource in trying to convince such reluctant consumers?

The real job of marketing is to be customer focussed. This does not mean 'making the customer like what we have got', instead it is about finding out what customers want and value or identifying their unsatisfied needs and helping the organization configure itself around this.

Good common sense can be applied here and there are many universal 'needs' which we can not only see around us, but also relate to personally. Being honest about the solution to these will make the product offering more relevant and the accompanying messages more authentic and believable. Sometimes though, we may come across a 'solution' to a problem which hasn't yet been identified. This would be classified in marketing terms as an unexpressed need; indeed how can we articulate a desire for something when it doesn't yet exist? An example might be text messaging: before it was invented we didn't know we 'needed' it, in fact had research been conducted at the time we would probably have got the answer, 'No, I don't need a new way of communicating, I have plenty already'.

'Solution' messages are about really testing your offering in a robust way and ascertaining if it is an actual answer or finding undiscovered 'need' in your audience and capitalizing upon this. Apply these practical aspects to your messages and you will be half-way towards real stickiness. Magner's understood the consumer need for real refreshment, so delivered it in a big way by having their cider poured into glasses crammed with ice. The product itself had remained unaltered, but the 'solution' was sufficiently appealing to boost brand share.

Needs analysis

To understand what your potential customers or prospects get from you and your business you need to go through the process of thinking about their expressed and hidden needs. We'll use the example of a travel agency to illustrate this.

Why do people need my travel agency? Think widely to begin with. What reasons do people have to travel? Examples might be for business, leisure, to broaden the mind, visit relatives abroad, deliver something by hand. A trip might have a specific purpose or be for relaxation, stress reduction, recuperation after illness or to meet new people.

Next, consider the destinations they may want to go to, do you have any inside knowledge of these places, have you been there yourself?

How might they like to travel, what alternatives are there and which criteria would they apply when deciding? Sometimes time is of the essence, so you'd choose to fly rather than sail; perhaps cost is a factor; or maybe the traveller wants to take in the landscape they pass through.

Finding the answers to some of these questions can give you insight into how much 'facilitation' you can add to the trip (this after all is part of the core skill of the travel arranger).

Exercise 6.1

Could you now begin to build some travel scenarios around the examples below? What headline messages might accompany them?

> 'Business travel throughout Europe, hassle free for the busy businessman'
>
> 'Blue is the colour, from the sky above to the sea below, cruise at your own pace'
>
> 'A road less travelled awaits the explorer... feeling adventurous?'

Try the same exercise now with an independent furniture store, online jewellery business or landscape gardener.

Follow this by applying the principles to your own business. These are the foundation stones for your own messaging campaign.

We talked about stickiness being a way of winning hearts and minds and have so far covered the logical, objective part of that equation, but what of emotion? What role can it play? As we have done earlier, let's break down 'emotion' into the component parts which matter.

Feelings

Great messages that stay in the memory do so because they provoke an emotional reaction in us: this might be happiness, sadness, regret, sorrow, elation, or many others. The strength of the emotion experienced can be a direct indicator of how long the message will stay in our consciousness. Happy childhood memories like a day on the beach are often underpinned by emotive feelings of closeness to our family.

> Charitable appeals attempt to engender strong emotions in us and many do so very successfully. The power and impact of a well-delivered package can result in many of us taking action. An iconic example of this phenomenon was at the Live Aid concert in 1985. Rock star David Bowie took the decision to cut his set short in order to show a film of starvation in Ethiopia, set poignantly to the music track 'Drive' by the Cars.
>
> The song had been a hit some time earlier so was familiar to the audience already. What no one expected is how apposite the lyrics became when set against the harrowing images. To this day, when the track comes on the radio the immediate association for those who were there is with the striking imagery.

This is an example of emotion at its most powerful, and though our own messaging is unlikely to reach such a pitch, it does help to illustrate how much impact we can make if our communication contains feeling.

Tread with caution as overuse of this intensely personal medium can damage your credibility. Be sincere and act with integrity rather than exploiting some highly emotive subject for commercial gain. Here are a couple of appropriately pitched emotion-generating messages.

If you sell hands-free kits for mobile phones something suitable might be the following:

> Home safe? Calling your loved ones from the car to say you're running late is considerate, without hands-free it's irresponsible.
> **www.homesafekits.com**

Perhaps you are service-based in your offering:

> Breathless! Pure adrenaline-pumping exhilaration with Laser Dingy sailing lessons @ Lakeside, call 01234 567 89.

There will be plenty of issues you communicate on which are just matter-of-fact work in progress, so use emotion sparingly for the things which really do stir your own passions.

Remember we all have a different threshold when it comes to showing emotion which might be based on our upbringing, environment or personality. We all know those who wear their heart on their sleeve as well as more reserved types, so try to take account of the fact we're not all the same. Too much emotion and you might come across as a bit 'limp', too little and you'll appear cold.

Trust

Trust is an important element in building brands and in the same way we can think of ourselves as a personal brand, which over time the people we communicate with will come to trust.

If this kind of relationship can be built, it is a great platform for stickiness because people will come back time and again to a source they have found to be reliable in the past.

The first noteworthy thing to mention is the phrase 'building trust'. In our business dealings, as in our private relationships, we begin in safe territory, sharing a little at a time. If you are trying to sell me a new product which has never been seen before, it is likely that I will take a small quantity to begin with on a trial basis. When I discover it does what you promised, I'll be more inclined to order more next time, so trust is built in small stages.

Even if we have been let down in a minor way with, say, a broken promise we tend to take this personally and very much to heart. Tough lessons like this stick with us. In business or in the communication process do everything you can to maintain trust and if you feel it slipping away for whatever reason, seek feedback to address the issue early.

Building a relationship is predicated on finding areas of common ground upon which mutual trust can begin to thrive. When we share the moral values or religious beliefs or political opinions of others, we tend to more easily put our faith in them as people. They are like us, so we trust them much more readily.

FIGURE 4 The trust thermometer

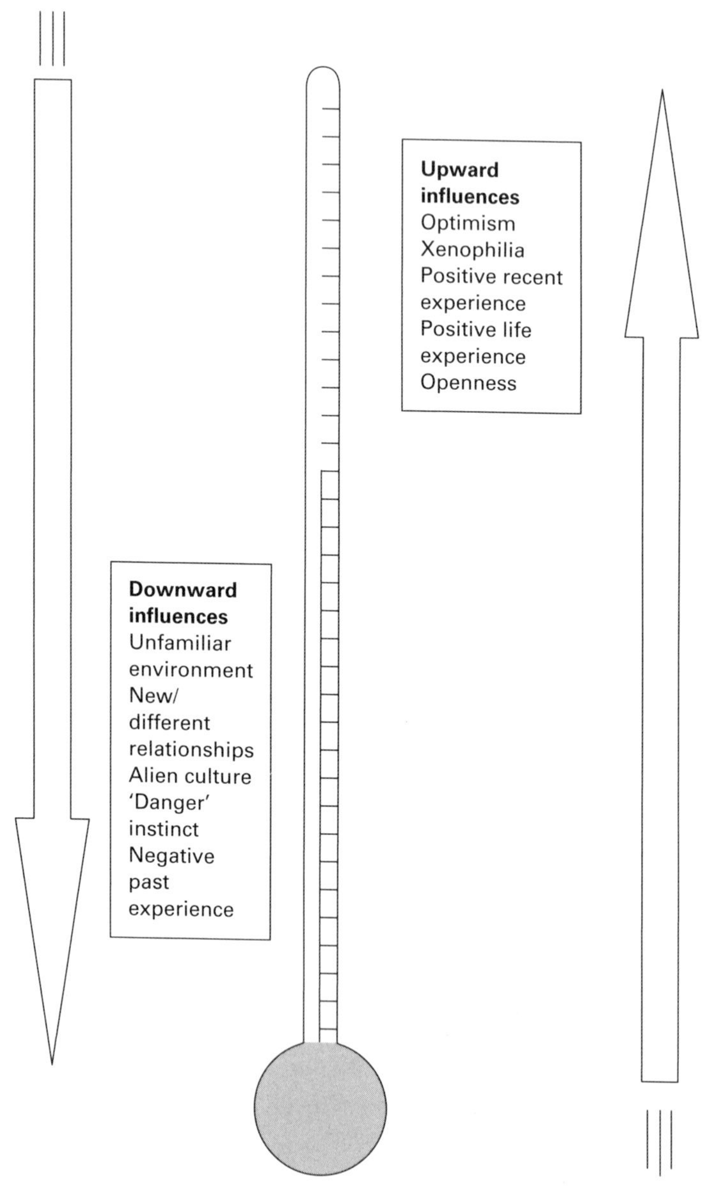

As the mercury rises we warm to people and situations (increased trust). As it falls we 'cool' (decreased trust).

Think about the factors which cause trust to rise or fall and use them to judge your outbound communication.

So, in the preceding pages we have covered both practical and emotional elements of stickiness. Keep these 'front of mind' and your messages will begin to ring loud and clear in the ears of your audience, causing them to choose to listen harder to what you have to say. In time this can result in your call to action being taken up.

FIGURE 5 Pick a sticky strand

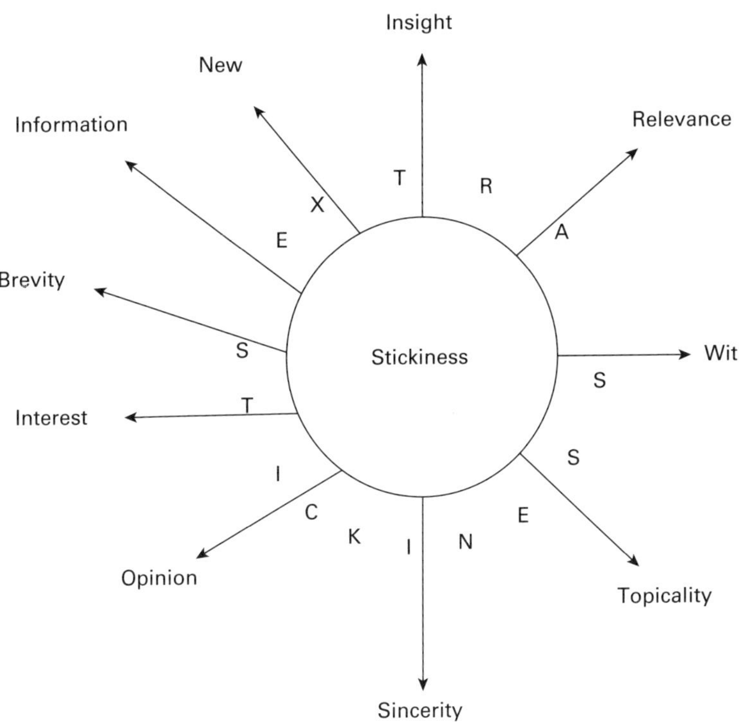

However sticky your current messages (inner circle) pull at any of the outer strands to increase impact and audience loyalty

Many of the common elements of 'stickiness' are shown here; the more you develop any or all of them, the more your messages will stick.

In short

- Sticky messaging is a product of the internet age, but can be applied across all communication streams.
- Relevance is driven by a combination of knowing your audience and staying up to date.
- Appeal to universal needs in humans and your messages will stick better.
- Really sticky messages make us *feel* something.
- Stickiness is a by-product of great two-way communication: remember to 'listen' as well as 'speak'.

Tip

Be emotional. Show how you are feeling and you will come across as warmer and more likeable.

Chapter Seven
Thoughts about blogging

Although we make frequent mention of blogging throughout this book it is potentially such a big part of any outgoing messaging campaign that this chapter is devoted solely to the topic.

If you have an existing blog or are thinking of setting one up, now is the time to take stock of its purpose, its value and its execution. We will examine all these things.

What are blogs?

It is more difficult to answer this question than one may have thought because the technical aspects of a blog, which allow any of us to post our thoughts and comments online, are simply the engine which drives the technology; after that, the content is as wide as we choose to make it. For this reason, some people use blogs to keep in touch with a community, maybe their family and friends or perhaps an interest group; others may blog for political reasons to have their opinions heard by a wider audience; or still more might choose to use a blog as a promotional tool. And these are just some of the uses.

Does it matter what other people are using blogs for, or should we just focus on our own game? The freedom which blogging allows us in expressing our opinions is fantastic if we decide to use this as a business tool, but as with all forms of communication, the marketplace for attention is very crowded indeed.

In the same way as we might pick up a weighty financial report only to be distracted a little later by a copy of a celebrity magazine which is also lying around, so the sheer volume of online content constantly pulls at the attention of our audience. Often it is the less worthy but more enticing content which wins out.

For this reason, we need to consider carefully the investment in time that we are thinking of making in our blog, and if we only approach it half-heartedly it would be better left alone: that time could more productively be spent on a different form of communication.

The decision of whether to blog or not might be made easier once we have considered what is involved in producing a really impactful blog. Broadly speaking, success is centred around having a clear sense of purpose, a strong idea of who the audience is and what we can do to appeal to them. This is added to the time and skill it will take to research, create and sustain compelling content. It sounds easy!

If blogging is going to be part of your communications strategy there is a clear stepped process which can help to get it off the ground, build its following and maintain a high level of interest over time.

1. Find out why

If you can't come up with an answer as to why you are blogging, it will never succeed. You may get the first few posts off the ground but without some clarity of mission the blog will very soon lose its way. One of the key things which audiences rely on is consistency and it is impossible to deliver this if you don't know what your purpose is.

From a practical point of view it is a good idea to compile your own 'statement of purpose'. Try to make this specific without taking all the creativity out of the intent. At the same time you need to have fleshed out the rationale so that you not only know just why you are doing this, but also have thought about the what and the how.

'I am blogging to generate more sales', is too limiting.

'I am blogging to build and inform an interested community of potential prospects with a view to creating loyalty to my brand and organization. I intend to use this to drive sales', is much more realistic and rounded.

One reason why our purpose statement needs to be about more than just selling is the fact that our audience is bombarded by conventional advertising from multiple sources all the time, and with a blog we want them to choose us of their own volition. It is unlikely they will do this if all we try to do is sell; there needs to be a genuine intent to satisfy a need, which might be for information and comment rather than an immediate transaction. However, all this loyalty building should have a pay-off somewhere down the line and we need to guard against our blog becoming something nice to have but with no call to action.

2. Pull don't push

The strategy which underpins our blog will help to shape it, and success is much more likely if we build our community of followers on the basis of genuine interest in their issues. What we're trying to do is have people elect to join and stay with us, rather than force them into reading what we want to output.

For a 'pull' strategy to work there has to be a clear, unambiguous and relevant link between the audience's unsatisfied need and our offering. It is no good blogging to a disparate audience and saying, 'Credit crunch getting you down, cheer yourself up with a pair of walking boots from OnMessage Boot Company'.

Instead you need to have built a community of walkers or potential walkers (those who we might be able to convince of the benefits of the hobby) and post something much more relevant, for example, 'Clocks go forward this weekend, longer days and better walking weather – the new Spring range of lightweight walking boots is available now from OnMessage Boot Company'. On its own this would make an ideal tweet, but on a blog it should be underpinned by broader, richer content, perhaps giving links to weather forecasting sites and tips on what to take when you head out.

3. Consider who is responsible

With a personal blog this is easy, but for an organization, even a small one, someone has to take overall responsibility for your output. There are many reasons for this, not least because you should have some plan in place which maps the level, frequency and breadth of your content, alongside some ideas of what you will actually be saying. Aside from this, when we consider the issue of consistency again, it is important that the audience does not detect a change in tone of voice.

One difficulty with blogging is that it can fill up any spare time we have and there is a cost to this, not least in terms of the lost opportunity to manage other aspects of our lives or businesses. Whoever the task of blogging is delegated to (most likely you) the parameters need to be strictly controlled.

4. Phase your blog in

The temptation at the beginning of a new blog is to 'feed the machine' at every opportunity. This is the point when we are bursting with ideas and generating rich content all the time. Remember, if your blog is to be successful you need to be in it for the long game and there is nothing more disappointing for new followers than to see the regularity of your posts dwindle away.

Start with the kind of frequency which is going to be realistic in the longer term, bearing in mind all the other things on your agenda.

5. Plan your time

To avoid creating a beast which may overwhelm you, allocate a strict amount of time to blog creation each week. If you find you have more time on your hands (which is frankly unlikely) you can always think about developing content for down the line.

Exercise 7.1 Developing a trailer

A good way of keeping an audience interested is to let them know your thought processes, so if you have set yourself some objectives with your blog, it is fine to outline these: it helps to trail the content you intend to develop. Don't get involved in too much detail here, you want to avoid being called to account by your audience in the future if you haven't delivered the specifics of what they expected. Instead, try to map out three months of topics. Begin by bullet-pointing them, then write a short sentence about each to tease your audience.

If you are committed to starting a blog there are many different ways of going about it. Firstly, when it comes to cost, it should be noted that many hosting services are freely available (look up **www.blogger.com** or **www.wordpress.com**; alternatively try a Google search and weigh up which is best for you). These services are becoming more sophisticated and rich all the time and will give step-by-step instructions on how to get started, including downloadable templates to give your blog a professional look and feel.

If this is beyond you, a raft of designers are available (again Google is the best place to start) who for a modest fee (for what amounts to a few hours' work) will get you up and running. As well as developing your blog, most will also throw in a Twitter set-up or other social networking site, so that you can begin to communicate across platforms.

Once the technical bit of the blog is done you can begin to think about content. The temptation for many small businesses is to begin developing content based on their product or service offering. Remember what we said earlier about too much sales push which can be off-putting. Make loyalty your aspiration at the start; the selling messages can follow later.

Think of the blog as a service to solve a 'problem' for your target audience. See Chapter 10 on taking a marketing approach.

A blog can take the form of a regular posting following a theme, a series of interesting but unconnected posts, or a more structured format like a newsletter.

If the latter, some time, thought and energy needs to be put into mapping out the key elements. Clues as to what might work well can be found in more traditional media.

Exercise 7.2 Building blocks of blogging

Think about a newspaper or magazine and some of the following elements may cascade from it:

- a short editorial to lead your readers in;
- a lead story – something topical and important;
- comment – the 'editor's' take on what is happening;
- multi-media – pictures and video to supplement your words;
- opinion pieces – thought-provoking articles putting your personal point of view;
- industry gossip – where appropriate;
- future gazing – speculation over what will happen next;
- pithy information – ten top tips;
- 'and finally...' – a lighter story to end on.

Consider how you might approach each of these elements with regard to your own messaging.

If you are new to blogging and all this advice seems overwhelming, you can begin the process in the territory of safe rehearsal by having a dry run. This means you don't have to risk exposure on the internet right away; instead over a pre-ordained period, say a month, you can trial the process of developing and writing content, collecting other assets like pictures and video, uncovering research sources (often other industry experts who may already be blogging) and pulling together a selection of posts, just to see if the process works for you.

If things don't pan out as planned you have the chance to go back to the drawing board, but what you will have on your side is that some content development will have taken place, giving you a good start to your blog when you go live.

Finally, for now, the important place to begin is by choosing your topic. This may sound obvious but lots of blogs fail because there has not been sufficient thought put in at this stage. Personal blogs often fall into this category. If you are just going to say what is on your mind today, some people will doubtless find it interesting, but if you go off on a completely different tack next time you post, they may not come with you.

Similarly, if you simply keep pushing out messages saying 'buy from me' you are unlikely to be successful, so choose something which is related to your business, something you are passionate about, and you will be at a good place to begin. If you own a restaurant, blog about your love of food, fresh local ingredients, new ways of cooking, how to present the 'restaurant look' at home, recipes which reflect the time of year (not just seasonal but one-offs like Halloween or Thanksgiving), and showcase a 'dish of the week' or a 'quick meal for busy people'.

Now, stop and think about your business: what was it that led you to become involved? When you think about your audience, how are they living their lives, what interests them about what you do? Content should begin to follow.

There is a lot of noise in the blogging arena but you already have the advantage over many bloggers inasmuch as you have considered your strategy, something which few others do. The majority of personal blogs are devised on an ad hoc basis and fall into many of the traps we have mentioned. A well-planned blog with rich content will grow over time, especially if supported by other communication channels.

Remember to cross-pollinate from one platform to another in terms of both content and promotion. Tweet about your blog contents and provide a hyperlink. Similarly, always mention your Twitter address when you are blogging. Apply this principle to whichever sites you are using.

In short

- Blogging is a great way of developing your business story.
- Many 'first-timers' fail through lack of planning.
- Treat blogging as a long game, don't rush at it.
- Drive your content by thinking about the main sections of a magazine.

Tip

Be yourself. This is what makes you different, unique and good to follow.

Section Three
Understanding customers: personal branding, segmentation and sales principles

- building a brand to deliver better messaging;
- segmenting an audience;
- developing relevance via marketing and sales.

Fantastic communication doesn't happen by chance: it is planned and built on solid foundations using established business principles. Here we look at how brands have become the ultimate shorthand messages, before examining ways of creating personal brands which speak volumes about our business.

Through applying solid sales and marketing thinking to underpin our messages we will better understand the stated and unfulfilled needs of our prospects and be able to target them much more precisely in future, delivering messages which are time-bound and relevant.

Chapter Eight
Building a brand to deliver better messaging

As we saw when we looked at stickiness, the ultimate in short messaging is the modern-day brand. Without opening its virtual mouth, the brand conveys all kinds of values, promises and propositions to consumers, many of which they are barely aware of on a conscious level. What matters is that they sell.

In this chapter we will look at what it takes to build a brand, the advantages of doing so and how the messages we develop can benefit from being associated with it. The easiest way to gain an understanding of how brands are created and sustained is to examine the topic from the viewpoint of consumer brands we are all familiar with. However, the 'rules' this sets up are just as valid when applied to small organizations, especially with regard to how they communicate.

By looking at the essential building blocks (or domains) of a brand, we will get an understanding of how to inject added value into our own market proposition.

Brand checking

To reinforce the power of branding, think about your own purchasing habits. Can you name the brands you buy when it comes to the following?

- petrol or gasoline;
- shoes;
- breakfast cereal;
- perfume or aftershave;
- coffee.

Are you confident you could tell the difference between these brands and their competitors if the label was taken off? If not, think hard about what motivates you to buy them.

Really successful brands build a caché around themselves; they become aspirational. Many of us are reluctant to own up to buying these products simply because of their label. Reasons we'd be likely to give would include 'hard-wearing' or 'well designed' or 'good quality'. The brand may well deliver these things, but often there is more to our motivation to buy.

This is easiest to understand at the prestige brand end of the spectrum where labels like Armani, Porsche and Jimmy Choo reside. But aside from us wanting to be like the glitterati there is a much more day-to-day side of branding that we are all drawn to. For example, do you buy supermarket own-brand coffee, or Nescafé? Would you opt for an unknown name in bottled water or choose Evian? The same can be said across the entire range of purchases we make.

Brands not only say something to us, but even more importantly, they say something about us.

How brands are built

Below are the building blocks of a brand. As you consider them, think how they relate to your offering and turn that thinking into a potential message for your prospects.

Start with a reliable product

You can't build your strategy on sand: you are going to have to be able to deliver some tangible benefit in whatever you are selling. Soap must remove dirt; waterproof boots must not leak; a watch must tell the time. There are certain fundamental functions that the product must deliver to give you any chance at all in the market. What is your product or service? What does it deliver?

Add value to consumers' lives

What extra will your customers get when they buy your brand? If it is the same as buying any comparable alternative then you have become 'commoditized', that is to say every competitor is seen as equal to you. There has to be a special something extra, if not in reality, then at least in perception. Maybe what you promise is soap which moisturizes the skin, waterproof boots for real adventurers, or a watch with built-in elegance. How provable any of these claims are is perhaps doubtful, but if the audience believe the promise their needs will be satisfied and you will have delivered value above and beyond the simple functionality of the product. Ask yourself where the added value is in your offering.

Stick with it

Whatever your proposition you need to develop it over time; brands are not built in a day. Even in the fast-moving world of technology it takes time, repetition and constant reinforcement of brand value to stoke up loyalty. Early brands like Quaker Oats, Juicy Fruit chewing gum and Tate & Lyle Golden Syrup have maintained their status in the marketplace through consistency and perseverance.

FIGURE 6 Adding value – avoiding commoditization

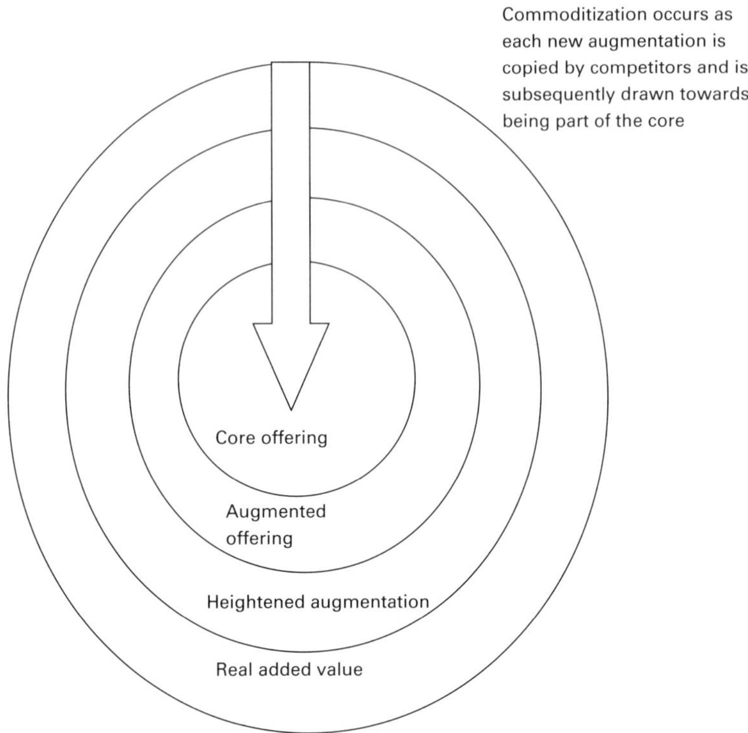

The core offering is essential to even be in the market

Each circle of augmentation seeks to add value

New elements of value eventually get drawn to the core

Value is sustained by continually adding elements which customers want to form new outer rings, eg longer opening hours, increased product range, faster delivery

The brands we develop may not be around for as long but the lesson we can learn from this is that branding is a long game. So think about how you will maintain momentum going forward.

Integration matters

Defining what a brand is going to convey is an important part of its development. Of equal significance is the set of surrounding communicators which say something about the brand itself; all of these have to be in line with the original proposition. Shell has tidy, well-maintained forecourts, staff are in uniform. Chanel no. 5 is boxed expensively, not sold in a paper bag. These supporting messages are key to the process of reinforcement and integration.

The comparison here is that if we have set ourselves up as a professional service, our targets won't expect to see messages full of spelling mistakes and typos.

Understanding the essential constructs of brands is part of the picture here, but it is only of use if it can inform us on how to build our own identity. The best way of doing this is to see our business as one which has a personality of its own, so we need an outline of the elements to think about and take some decisions on. There are five domains for brand personality.

Creativity

How 'out there' are you, how wild, gregarious and whacky? Some brands like Google (see below) and Vivienne Westwood are edgy, different and idiosyncratic. This suits their personality and what they are trying to convey, but it wouldn't fit easily with a firm of solicitors or a financial institution.

It's not that 'creative' is good and 'workmanlike' is bad; the decision is much more about where you sit along that line. Decide this in tandem with the purpose of your business, the people in it and your customers' expectations. The more creative you are the greater the likelihood of using chatty, conversational language in your posts; right at the edges you might expect slang, patois or street talk. When Google changed their privacy policy they drew users attention to it with the banner: 'This stuff is important.'

Risk

Closely associated with the first domain is how much of a risk-taker your brand personality is.

Being devil-may-care and maverick can look appealing from the outside, but it does have its attendant stresses and strains, not least the potential for reputational damage.

Case study – Virgin

When Virgin Mobile launched in a competitive arena they vowed to do their business differently. They would occasionally hold staff parties which sometimes resulted in revellers making it into the pages of the press for their antics. Far from causing damage to the good name of the brand, these incidents acted like a recruitment drive with queues of people lining up with a desire to work for such a 'feel-good' company.

Age

You don't need to put a defined number on the age of the brand, but having a sense of its life stage is important. Remember we are thinking of our organization as a person here: it's not about how long we have been trading but how we want to be seen. We might think of Virgin Mobile as being around 25, Mercedes Benz is probably mid-forties, Titleist might be 30-ish.

The 'voice' of these brands is often reflective of how their owners perceive them. Outbound messages are written and delivered in a manner which is congruent with the level of maturity they are trying to convey.

Price

How much you charge can send a powerful signal to purchasers about what they are getting. In sales and marketing terms, price is the issue most often misunderstood. When Stella Artois used the copy line 'reassuringly expensive', what did that say to consumers? The message was there to let Stella drinkers know they were in an exclusive club of people who could afford the premium lager. They were associating their product with words like 'rare', 'precious' and 'desirable', all good attributes to have.

Creative brand building – Stella Artois

Stella Artois used a variety of treatments to reinforce their message. Common elements tied the individual advertisements together to form a campaign. These included a retro feel, a lilting soundtrack and a gentle wit.

In one the peasant is taking his crop of flowers to market and stops off at a tavern for food. With no money to pay, he agrees the fee of two bunches of flowers for his baguette, but on seeing the barman pour a Stella decides he must have one of these as well. The closing shot is of the peasant quaffing his lager and as the camera pans out we see the tavern festooned in the entire crop of thousands of flowers.

An alternative classic brand builder involves hundreds of skating priests. One of the youngest is sent on a mission to secure a crate of Stella, but on his return he falls though a hole in the ice. In the ensuing hilarious bedlam the boy is saved but the lager drifts away under the ice. Through facial expression alone (no dialogue is used) the senior priest instructs the boy to dive again to save the beer.

The rarity and 'specialness' of the drink is reinforced in both commercials.

When you believe in what you're selling, set a price point that reflects its true value and take it to the market, the bracket you have put it into conveys its own message to prospects. A silver service restaurant run by a top chef is never going to be cheap; on the other hand there is no shame in advertising your diner as serving 'fresh homemade dishes at good value prices'.

'Relative' value

Finally, to complete the picture of your business's personality, picture it in terms of the relationship you want it to have with its customers. If it were their relative, would it be a trusted uncle (as in a mortgage product, for example), or maybe a teenage cousin (a games company). If not family, would it be a best mate in the bar, a wise old mentor or an eccentric acquaintance.

Any of these descriptions is valid according to what you want to convey; the point is that when you know in conceptual terms 'who' your brand is, you will not only have a good idea of what it would say, but importantly, how it might say it. This can go a long way to governing the tone of voice you use in blogs, web, tweets and more.

Brand case studies

To be different and stand out in the right way is a huge source of competitive advantage, something most businesses seek. Branding can help us do that via the creation of a brand personality. The following case studies contrast the attributes of different brands by looking at their 'personalities'. After reading them, stop and think about how your 'personality' is currently portrayed through your messaging and whether you could do more to emphasize your best features.

Case study – Google

Regarded as the premier search engine, Google has distinct characteristics which are attributable to its look, feel and functionality. Back stories about the company abound and despite some bad press it has largely managed to weather this storm.

Brand strength comes primarily from the fact that it works so well, delivering accurate, relevant results in a fraction of a second. Without this efficiency we wouldn't stick with it.

The plain simple home page looks different to its earlier competitors which were cluttered with banner advertisements and clashing colours.

Google is self-effacing and prepared to take risks. Regularly the central home page logo is cannibalized in honour of a particular event, often an artist's birthday or to trumpet a national holiday (these are called Google Doodles). The essence of the brand is pushed and pulled this way and that for our entertainment; this says they don't take themselves too seriously.

Behind the scenes Google sounds like a great place to work: there are rumoured to be fireman's poles between floors in the offices and an unofficial mantra underpinning the mission statement which states 'Don't be evil', a rather consoling statement in these days of corporate corruption.

Case Study – Walmart

One of the world's largest retailers, famed for an emphasis on low price and high-quality service, Walmart strives to preserve its homespun roots image. Having been started by Sam Walton the espoused values of the brand are all about 'ordinary folk doing extraordinary things'. This message is marbled through the training of employees and forms part of the organizational manifesto.

Other brand values are built around connecting with customers (stores have greeters at the door), and part of policy is 'the 10 foot rule' (whenever a customer comes within 10 feet of an associate they are to look them in the eye, greet them and ask if they can help).

Customer service is further underpinned by the 'sundown rule' which says don't put off until tomorrow what you can do today (particularly if this means delivering a service to a customer).

Walmart's personality is one of a big player with an even bigger heart. An important part of consolidating this stance is via written communication, but the real game-changer is having the staff bought in to the ethos so that there is integration of communication, each aspect reinforces the next. The advantage to customers is the low price brought about by their buying power, but this is not at the expense of service: there will always be a metaphorical 'arm around the shoulder'.

Exercise 8.1 Your brand proposition

In a year's time if you were asked to write up a similar case study of your own brand, how would it look?

What values would it live by and, most importantly of all, who would it be in terms of personality? The closer we get to understanding this, the more easily our messages will flow and our tone will become consistent which is an important part of being sticky.

In short

- Brands are the ultimate way of conveying short messages.
- No one builds a brand overnight, but the process has to start somewhere.
- Think of your own brand as having a personality.
- Consistency is the watchword of good branding.

Tip

Be curious. Find out what's going on in as many spheres of life as possible, reflect your knowledge as part of an intelligent brand.

Chapter Nine
Segmenting an audience

When taking the brief for a new advertising campaign the copywriter asked the client, 'What kind of people come in here?'

'All sorts', came the reply.

Naturally all sorts of people walk through the doors of any business – tall, short, blonde, brunette – but there is something a bit more fundamental which binds this 'all sorts' together and sets them apart from the 'all sorts' who walk into the store down the road.

This is much easier to grasp when we begin to think about particular kinds of business. What are the 'all sorts' like who walk through the doors of the Porsche dealership? To begin with, they're the kind of 'all sorts' who are doing okay in life, they've made some money along the way. But their common attributes run much deeper than this.

If asked to picture someone in a Porsche, do you think of a middle-aged businessman or a young blonde girl? In real life you have probably seen both. For them and the thousands of others who buy Porsches, the vehicle has attributes which fit their idea of an ideal car for the price. Bear in mind that we have to compromise. There is a trade-off between what we might really desire and what we can afford; this is a factor behind every purchasing decision we make.

If you drive a small Fiat, your dream car may be the Porsche but you are not in that segment of the market because you cannot afford to be. It equally holds true that many of the Porsche drivers may aspire to something 'better' too. But aside from price as a purchasing criterion, markets aren't self-segmenting. They are driven by influencers, the messages planted in the heads of potential customers which over time lead them towards one purchase rather than another. This is not an accident.

If we fail to work out who might want to buy our product or service, we stand little chance of being able to deliver messages that hit home. This chapter is about working through who your 'all sorts' are, or to give it its proper term, segmentation.

We will look at the fundamental principles and examine down-to-earth practical ways in which we can think about segmenting our own audiences, tracking their preferences and considering the messages which will not only entertain, amuse and inform them, but also drive them to choose us over the competition.

Segmentation is an important marketing tool and will be invaluable in helping you make sense of the audience for your product or service. It is only when we have a deep understanding of the common attributes which drive these people that we will maximize our effectiveness to message them with relevance.

Who are your prospects?

Putting the international car brands to one side for a moment, who are your 'all sorts'? This is a vital question for all businesses, but particularly important for the smaller enterprise. Some sole traders have little or no understanding of their customers, so they lump them all together without unpicking what motivates their shopping habits. Of course this isn't really very important when times are good.

One of the defining traits of boom is that demand outstrips supply. Put simply, there are more customers for any particular product than there are products on the shelf. Why should it matter if we don't stop and think about the people who purchase, as long as they keep coming we keep making money?

But we know that economic conditions are not static, they are cyclical, and if you don't know why you are successful during the good times (by having an understanding of both who your customers are and what you have which attracts them) you will flounder in the bad times (when supply outstrips demand).

Sorting out your 'all sorts'

In order to develop messages which hit home harder with our target audience and stand more chance of motivating them to do our bidding (buy something, share our opinion, support our ideology), we need to get to know them better. So, instead of thinking of them as a disparate collection of individuals who have encountered us by chance, let us begin to consider their common characteristics by examining some of the ways in which we can segment them.

For pragmatic purposes we have split this into two sections covering both simple and complex segmentation. The reason for this is that many marketing theorists talk as though every business has a limitless budget to spend on research and focus groups. The reality for many small businesses is we must conduct our 'research' much more by observation on a day-to-day basis; often it is no less valid for this. To help illustrate each form of segmentation we will look at examples of products in the marketplace which have distinct characteristics. When reading through the major types of segmentation, think how it relates to your customer base or audience profile.

Simple segmentation

Gender

The obvious divide between the sexes will be over clothing and cosmetics, each group buying distinctly different types. However, many more products and services will be heavily biased towards gender. Fresh-cut flowers are bought more by women (although the gap is narrowing); men buy more newspapers. Both sexes buy cars although where some models are concerned there is a distinct bias towards one gender or the other.

Apply common sense to your own offering: is it more likely that men or women will purchase, or is it not gender-sensitive?

A word of caution: over time these biases can change in relation to a whole host of factors. For instance 50 years ago there was virtually no market for men's cosmetics; now it is a boom business with ever-increasing sales of anti-ageing products.

Age

Again, be careful with this one: we can sometimes make false assumptions. The commonsense rule applies once more. In the travel market, cruises tend to be the choice of more mature holiday-makers; snowboarding and extreme sports usually fit at the other end of the age spectrum. There are many more products and services which cut across the age ranges, such as river fishing, painting and classical music; these are areas which tend to have fewer boundaries. It is also true that the 'old are getting younger', so more and more citizens of retirement age are engaging with new technologies which were at one time thought of as the preserve of the young.

Writing for the right age group

One of the most difficult challenges any business faces is writing in the language their audience will most likely engage with, especially if there are multiple groups to appeal to.

We've used the fishing example before, so for this exercise let us stick with that. Write a couple of short sentences to position your angling supplies business at the top end of the market (premium-priced), firstly for a mature audience, then for a much younger segment.

Resist the temptation to read the suggested answers below, before making your own attempt.

Mature customers

Lazy, sultry, summer days. You, the riverbank, the sunshine and the sport. Best-quality angling supplies from experts who know. Order online for next (lazy) day delivery www.anglyjangly.com – WARNING – may ruin your 'one that got away' stories!

Young customers

Big fish – big battle. Win every time with an angling advantage – www.anglyjangly.com. Sucker him in, 'hook, line and sinker'!

Geography

This element of customer behaviour was once much more significant – when there was less social mobility. Many goods tended to be sourced locally, from food through to hardware. However, in many commodity markets there is literally a world of choice. Internet shopping has broken down the old boundaries; now we can and do source our goods from anywhere.

This provides a great opportunity for many businesses.

Going global – a retailer's tale

I've always been mad about music, so my first foray into business was to open a shop selling instruments. It did okay, but to a large extent it was limited by geography. Local people would come and buy from me but that wasn't enough to make a decent living.

Over time I specialized in saxophones, buying and selling second-hand ones alongside the new, ending up with lots of stock and a limited customer base which was hardly a recipe for success. Then eBay came along and transformed the market and my fortunes. I was able to take my business not just to the next town, but far beyond. I was suddenly a global player, albeit a very small one. The expertise I'd amassed alongside all those saxophones meant I was in a niche which aficionados the world over would be prepared to seek out.
(Simon Catherall)

Businesses which are less affected by globalization tend to be in the service sector. If we have a problem with the plumbing we're going to get the local firm in; similarly if we join a gym the likelihood is it will be within a 12 mile radius of work or home (outside this distance we are unlikely to use it regularly).

However, even if you are not selling consumer goods, don't dismiss the global market: there may be many people out there who are willing to pay for your expertise. It might be something which can be dispensed over the internet.

We will further examine this phenomenon of globalization later, in Chapter 15, and look at some golden rules of cross-cultural communication as well as thinking about how we can tailor our messages to different groups in order to maximize success.

Complex segmentation

Because our buying motivations are based on many factors, it is sometimes hard to fathom why one choice is made over and above another. There is a school of thought which says that everything we buy takes us a little closer to the person we aspire to be, which is not a bad rule of thumb to consider when constructing messages. They should contain an element of aspiration or the potential to fulfil an ambition.

Sometimes we can roll up a number of the simple segmentation factors and begin to get a better overall picture of who we are talking to.

Demographic

Age and gender can play a part in defining demographic groups, but to complete the picture we are likely to include additional information like income group, occupation, education and perhaps even religion or race. This type of segmentation is getting more sophisticated all the time but to do it scientifically requires substantial investment in data collection and analysis. Sometimes our instincts will take us part of the way down this road, without having to spend on market research.

Exercise 9.1 Supermarket sweep

Over the course of a month visit a range of supermarkets in your area. Compare the products on offer, the store layout and consider the kind of people they might attract. Could you outline a pen picture of a typical shopper in each store, outlining their characteristics? What do they wear, how old are they, what kind of vehicles are in the car park? Whether you have a local or global perspective, could you do this exercise by making an educated guess? In the following markets, how would you typify the customers of these supermarkets?

- UK: Waitrose versus Asda.
- USA: Walmart versus Winn Dixie.
- Spain: Dino Sol versus Mercadona.
- China: Vanguard versus Wu-Mart.

We need to be careful here as we are basing our 'assumptions' on experience rather than science, but by getting an idea of the kind of customers who shop in each we are honing our commonsense segmentation skills.

The more you can discover about the lifestyle and buying habits of your customers, the greater the likelihood that you will be able to target products and messages to them.

Psychographic

A step further on from conventional demographic segmentation is the attempt to unravel buying behaviours based on things like lifestyle and personality. Here it may be useful to think of the typical clothing stores you might find in your high street.

Are there certain shops you would never go in? If so, is it because the style of their clothes is too old, too young, too fashionable, too dowdy, too outrageous, too casual? We often reflect our personality back on the world by the way we dress; it says something about us. So, in the same way as before, it can help if we are able to get under the skin of the personality type of our customers.

If you have a business which makes hand-crafted silver jewellery to a particular quirky design, your customers will very likely share a desire to be different. This may show itself in their clothing, ideology or views. When you can tap into this precisely, you have great insight to the type of message they might respond to.

We began this chapter by talking about 'all sorts'. If you still think your customer base or potential audience is made up of 'all sorts' who have no common bond you will be missing the trick of targeting your messages with precision.

On the other hand, if you have started to consider more seriously the benefits of honing down on a segment, there is a way of developing this knowledge into a set of useful attributes for your product or service. This is done via positioning maps, which are a useful tool often used in marketing. Look at the maps in Figure 7 and think about where you would plot your business or message. Don't be confined to the parameters which are outlined here; you can develop your own maps based on attributes that are most relevant to your type of business.

FIGURE 7 Positioning maps

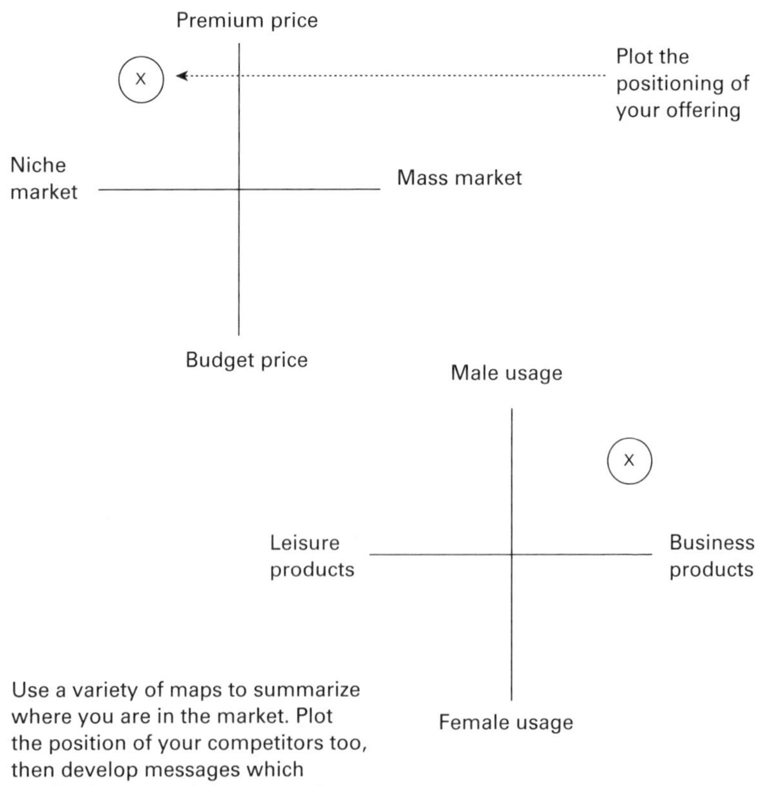

The future of segmentation

There are always surprise trends and cults in business and in life generally. Think back to your youth and it might have been Hula-Hoops, Clackers or Hot Wheels, but many of the big hits of the past have come about by design rather than accident. Deep understanding of unfulfilled need allied to accurate audience segmentation has driven clear messaging via advertising and promotional messages, resulting in sales throughput.

The power of segmentation in this context cannot be ignored and it is getting tighter and more sophisticated with every passing year. As 'innocent' consumers we may not even have noticed the way this has been facilitated, but the truth is accurate segmentation relies on data, and tons of it.

Tracking who buys what has become a science which retailers and manufacturers have taken to a whole new level. Data is collected via our credit and debit card transactions showing where we shop, but more than this our every purchase can be mapped if we use a store loyalty card. Online the information is even richer: it's not just what we buy but how we express our preferences. Not only can our purchasing habits be tracked, but also our attitudes, beliefs and values. This is because every time we search online or click 'like' on a social networking site a new part of our personal picture is being collated. It is no coincidence that banner advertising is relevant to what is on our mind.

The irrefutable truth is that we buy what our friends buy or like (whether real or cyber friends), so if they recommend something (by 'liking' it online) we are more likely to be drawn to it.

How does this help us in a small enterprise? Firstly, it points towards a way of thinking which we have discussed here already, that of understanding our customers holistically, not just what they buy from us, but other purchases they make, their lifestyle, their preferences. Secondly, all the data which is being mined can be useful to us if we tap into it, and in lots of ways we can, for free. Increasingly the big players are telling us 'people who bought this also bought this...', so we can see the factual data for ourselves.

Twitter segments

Twitter is a great way of tracking attitudes and likes. If you can discover who your customers follow, besides you, and then watch what those members tweet for a while, you will gain great insight into what turns your prospects on. When you understand them better you can message them in a more appropriate way. This is a running theme for developing our messaging, and social networks can provide a rich vein of information to help us achieve insight.

The future is likely to be even more exciting as we increasingly become aware of not just what transactions are likely to be made and when, but also the underlying buying psyche, the motivation to purchase. The more closely we can map this against our blogs and tweets, the greater the likelihood that we will hit our prospects at the right time with the right message.

In short

- 'All sorts' is too broad a term for your customers; work out which sorts they are.
- Look for similar characteristics which bind your customers together.
- Try to look beyond the obvious: what is it about their lifestyle which is common? (Hippies come in all ages!)
- Use segmentation to drive your positioning: what does this customer group value?

Tip

Observe. Become a people and world watcher: the more connections you make, the better attuned your messaging will be.

Chapter Ten
Developing relevance via marketing and sales

Segmentation is an age-old marketing tool which has stood us in good stead for many years of commerce. It is a sound basic principle which helps us understand why certain people buy certain things, and if we apply the theory that 'clusters' of like-minded individuals will share the same tastes, we are better able from the supply side to understand their needs.

This chapter consolidates what we have learned about the constructs of good segmentation and applies that knowledge in a way which will bring real relevance to your offering and a much deeper understanding of the elements which need to be part of the sales message. Applying some classical marketing theory to the topic of messaging helps us understand the perceived value in what we're selling, and that will drive our outbound communication.

Applying the 'so what?' test

Whatever product or service you are offering it is important to know where it fits in the jigsaw of people's lives. When we understand this we can develop a key insight to effective messaging, that of relevance; as we saw earlier this is an essential ingredient of stickiness. If we give a clear reason why you should buy this now and it chimes with other things which are going on in your life, it makes sense that you will more readily respond. If, instead, consumers read our message and say, 'So what?' we have lost the battle.

On a simple level this might be something like retailing sunglasses at the start of summer or developing offers which match a financial need. Notice how food retailers have begun to package the meal for two at home. If they simply advertised the component ingredients and their prices, far fewer of us would make the connection. Instead, rather than advertise the food, they focus on the experience. A TV commercial (which is just like any other message a business might send) on a Friday night, promising 'dinner for two at home for £15', contains many subliminal messages:

- Cheaper than eating out (in these cash-strapped times).
- No effort getting ready (you can relax at home).
- Ease of preparation (high-quality convenience food means little preparation or washing up).
- A treat (for the end of the week, without breaking the bank).

So the challenge is, what are your customers doing right now, what have they planned for the weekend, how could your product or service make their lives easier or enrich them in some way?

Pangs of hunger

The modern deli, sandwich store or coffee shop is a triumph of 'relevance'. Places like Pret a Manger and Starbucks have thought through the lives and lifestyles of their customers and provide what is needed according to the time of day.

Merchandizing is no accident, and every couple of hours the emphasis changes from a cycle of early-morning goods like pastries and bacon baps, through mid-morning snacks like cakes and biscuits, onwards to lunchtime with soup and sandwich offerings. Many of these stores are re-merchandized up to half a dozen times a day. Their relevance is no accident.

When you've worked through the way your customers live their lives you can begin the process of putting together a message so relevant that they'll find it hard to ignore. To help with this process here are five tips for honing the skill of relevance.

1. Keep your eyes and ears open

Messages can be relevant because of their time sensitivity. Responding to who has just won an Oscar, a great sporting victory, changes in the weather or the launch of a new smartphone means catching the audience when they are thinking about these things. Make sure you link your message to the event for maximum impact.

'Even the new iphone hasn't got an "aroma-app". Smell how good our fresh-baked bread is @ 42 High Street, every morning from 7 a.m. – what a way to start your day!'

'So the Aussies won the cricket – join in their celebrations with a beach Barbie down under – flights and packages from $399 – visit www.downunderbarbie.au.'

And remember, it's not only what's happening now which matters: if you can guess ahead and anticipate the future, you can be first to the punch when an event occurs. Think about what is coming up in the news, entertainment or sporting calendar and prepare messages for a number of contingencies. In the Oscars example you can get the nominees weeks in advance, so develop a range of responses according to what wins and be the first to tweet or blog, the very second the results are announced.

2. Tap into trends

The news agenda is notoriously flighty, what is huge today is out of vogue tomorrow. It is no good tweeting about the state of the economy on a day when a big health scare story has broken, so make sure you know what is trending, right now. Pull together your own 'pod' of sources and try to ensure it is the same as the media your audience follows. Subscribe to a relevant publication, gather some 'favourites' in your bookmarks and add these to the best Twitter has to offer, allied to your most-visited blogs.

Next time you are in the local newsagent take 30 seconds to scan the racks. The big personalities and most popular gossip will sing out at you from the front pages. According to what business you're in you don't necessarily need to join this bandwagon but it is unforgivable to be oblivious to it.

3. Follow the big boys

You may have found your niche in a particular market but remember that the mass media is exactly that: a source of information and entertainment for the masses. You don't need a horde of journalists, writers and investigators working for you directly, instead you can pick up on what is being written about by observing the big beasts of the media world.

The same word of warning applies here: the news agenda is so fast-moving now that you have to be thinking of immediate responses to what is going on. A thoughtful opinion piece which you have devised for your blog may be irrelevant by the time you publish.

4. Consolidate your data

Get organized! Develop a virtual filing system where you can store all the good stuff you come across. Give folders names which are relevant to your business. If you're involved in technology they may be things like 'What's new?', 'Competitor info', 'Coming soon' or 'Expert opinion'.

Periodically (at least once a month) scan through the folders, throw away anything which is redundant and take note of the items which matter; these will help to drive your content creation down the line.

5. Keep asking questions

Use Twitter and other social media to do instant market research on what is 'in' and what is not. Test out the validity of your ideas by asking direct questions in your messages, or post something thought-provoking like an undiscovered YouTube gem and see how many 'likes' you get.

When a big story breaks try to second-guess the questions your audience might be thinking about and reflect this in your posts; for example: 'Is it just me or is everyone else confused about quantitative easing?'

Try something new (test marketing)

You don't need to be inventing new products to take to market all the while; instead the challenge is to find new ways of packaging an existing idea and developing a message to make it appealing. If you get it right it will develop its own momentum and become relevant as a consequence.

This is very much in line with other advice we've given on lifestyle. Stop thinking about product and consider what it will do for people. If you are selling someone a camera they aren't buying a device which will take photographs, they are investing in a method of capturing memories. We've all heard the phrase, 'the soundtrack of our lives': steal this idea and use it to enhance the camera proposition, for example, 'The Niko S20 – helps you create the pinboard of your life'. Try to make these connections for your own offering.

Developing a sales proposition

The relevance we have talked about here is a key part of understanding what messages will hit home with our prospects, but there is more to it than that.

Knowing what makes people buy is important if we're going to construct outbound communications that really motivate an audience towards us. Of course this is not restricted to consumer goods. We have talked before about our desire to sometimes sell an ideology or opinion. Often we are seeking to persuade and sales technique is at the heart of this.

Don't forget that there are many unexpressed elements in the purchasing process. We might try on a jacket in a store, look in the mirror and think, 'Hey, this is really me!' but we'd be more reluctant to admit this to our friends; instead the tendency is to wait for them to pass a compliment. If it really is true that many of our purchases take us closer to the person we'd like to be, this can be much too personal a thing to admit to. So, when market researchers compile their weighty reports on behalf of their clients, there is often much more going on beneath the surface, which respondents don't own up to.

Getting to unexpressed wants can be difficult, partly because of this lack of real honesty in responding to research, and partly because there are sometimes products which come to market that are so revolutionary we didn't know we needed them until they arrived.

The unknown unknowns!

In-car satellite navigation has revolutionized travel, meaning that we need never get lost again. Before it, we may have had an unexpressed desire to always know where we were going and the wisdom at the time would have suggested we buy a map. You can't express a desire for something if you don't know what it is!

Add to this the fact that if you ask existing loyal customers what they'd like from you, the most likely answer is 'More of the same, but a bit cheaper'. This focus on price in our purchasing is a natural function of wanting to get a good deal, but often it detracts from the real process which is going on when we make a purchasing decision.

The real reason people make a purchasing decision is based instead on value. We ask, what are we getting in return for what we pay? Why is this important and relevant to our messaging? The answer is simple: understand what really drives people to purchase and your messages will be tailored as a consequence. Fail to grasp this and all you're left with is claiming you are the cheapest in town.

The recognized foundations of good marketing are based on the Seven P's and this can teach us a lot about where to look for inspiration in our communication. By way of explanation, the first six of the P's concentrate on the elements that would add value to a proposition; these can be compared like-for-like with our competitors. The final P is price, which we divide the other ones by to deliver a value proposition.

FIGURE 8 The value equation

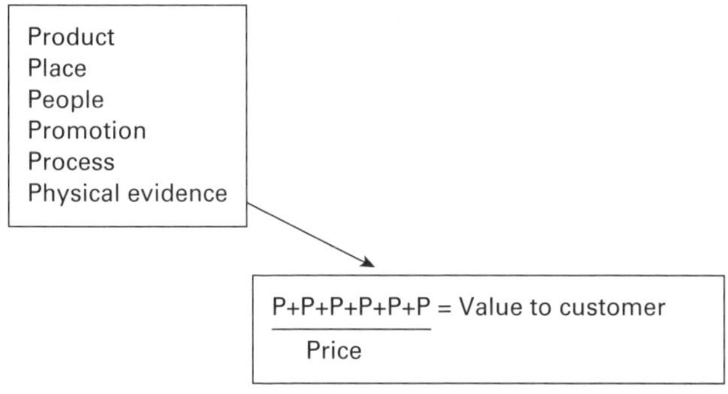

How much value is defined based on the 'offering' (6Ps) divided by the price

The 'offering' can be assessed across a range of domains (the 6Ps of product, place, people, promotion, process and physical evidence)

Only when the 'offerings' are identical from two suppliers does the price become a factor

Good marketers increase value by **adding** to the top line (6Ps) **not** reducing the price

Value-based elements and the messages they generate

Product

It is fundamental that you have a product (or service) you believe in and can talk about with passion and positivity. We have seen before that whatever its function, it has to be able to perform it, otherwise you are not in the market. A car for example needs an engine, wheels, seats and a braking system; beyond this there may be a host of other features such as air con, sound system and electric windows, all of which enhance the core offering.

So the challenge is how you describe your product: what is it that may appeal to potential customers? Instead of thinking just about the features, turn these into benefits: what does the consumer get by purchasing your offer (see the camera example above)?

Place (availability)

Aside from the physical attributes of what you're selling there are many more things which will make prospects buy from you. The first of these added-value elements is called place. This is not only the physical premises but also your hours of business; it adds up to availability. If you are open late when others in your marketplace have gone home, this will give you an advantage.

In a restaurant you can increase your 'place' over competitors by making sure you have more staff on at busy times, boosting your availability.

People

In a store or other sales outlet where face-to-face transactions take place it is easy to understand the role of people. Whoever is at this interface needs to reflect the offering: hairdressers are often creative and zany with their own looks, financiers dress smartly and have clean nails; there are countless examples of this congruity. Whether you have a physical high street presence or a virtual store online, how the people come across must reflect the offering. We discussed the principle of integration in Chapter 8 when we looked at branding and this is just as important when it comes to people as any other aspect which can convey a message, no matter how subliminal, to our audience.

Promotion

The messages associated with promotional offers need to be consistent with all the rest of your product's attributes. Rather than go down the route of offering the cheapest in town, try messages which major on lifestyle and added value, for example, 'Buy these five food items and get a free bottle of wine to complete your dining experience'. The important thing about good promotions is that the customer places a high value on what you offer, but it costs you little; for example, the price they would pay for a bottle of wine at restaurant prices is much more than it costs you when you purchase in bulk from your wholesaler.

Process

Make it easy to browse and buy and you will attract more business. Part of your messaging should reflect this is the case. Simple things like, 'All orders received by 4 p.m. are despatched the same day', are part of the process offering. How can you simplify your processes from the customer perspective? More importantly, how are you going to let them know that it is easier to buy from you?

Physical evidence

Company logos, staff uniforms and signage are all a part of the physical evidence of a business and its offering. Once again it is important that this is consistent, and the form it may take in our messages is the design of our blog (subtle and stylish, or zany and outlandish, according to what we are trying to portray), or in the use of logos or other standard intellectual property.

These are all important elements when we are developing our communications: if we have a greater sense of why people might buy our product or service, and a clear understanding of what it does for them (makes them look good, stops them getting lost etcetera), we are much more able to incorporate that into the message.

Before we finish with the topic of sales messages, it is worth looking at some principal reasons for the purchases we all make. We may not always do this knowingly, but the rationale is sound nevertheless.

Utility

Many things we buy because they do something, they have some usefulness in our lives. A spade is a good tool if you want to dig the garden, a kettle helps us make tea. There are some things in life which we just consider as essentials. Although it is good to stress in our messages how useful what we're selling is, don't get fooled into thinking this is all that matters. Many people may choose the basic spade, but others will go for the top-of-the-range branded variety; the reason is probably to do with seeing themselves as expert or professional gardeners, so why wouldn't they treat themselves to the best?

Even the most basic items in life can be dressed to appear both essential and appealing.

Narcissism

You won't get many people owning up to this as a buying motivation but it would be a foolish businessman who ignored it. We live in a world which is bombarded by images of youth and beauty and are continually told this is what we should seek. No matter how down-to-earth a person you are, we all share a desire for inclusion so may fall prey to this trick. You may not be selling a product which will make people more beautiful, but remember that one of the prime buying motives we've mentioned is that we are all striving to get closer to the person we'd like to be. Offer that promise in whatever you are selling and you will be hard to resist.

Desire

Aesthetics play a part in our buying decisions: some things are just inherently beautiful. This signals the need for us to present our business in the most attractive way possible. That means not only should pack shots be professional and appealing, but the words we use to describe our wares should match too. This idea can be applied across a whole range of goods to make them more desirable. Think about how menus are written: they frequently make the dishes sound much more appealing than anything we could cook at home. Even sandwiches sound better if they're described as 'freshly cut sandwiches'. Add desire to whatever you sell.

Aspiration

The problem with price wars is that they take little account of aspiration; it's as if everybody wants everything as cheaply as they can get it. Naturally we don't want to feel ripped off, but sometimes spending a large amount on a single item is part of us reinforcing our worth (to ourselves and the world). This is why cars have become the ultimate status symbol: they are a shorthand way of judging our relative worth against those around us. Make your goods or services an aspiration and you will increase consumer desire.

Trust

Some purchases are made on a repeat basis. There can be many reasons for this, but it is fair to say that trust is built over time and, as we have established, can be a core element of brand value. If you run a high street butcher and I get consistently good meat from you, I will return time and again. Even when the purchasing cycle is longer the same applies, so if we believe the carpet warehouse gave us a good deal, turned up on time, fitted well, cleared up afterwards and left us with a serviceable and attractive floor covering for five years, we will be inclined to return when it's getting worn out. If you are going to build the word 'trust' into your messaging, make sure you can deliver against it.

Value

Finally we come back to value once more. The exercise with the Seven P's which we looked at earlier describes how value can be built; just make sure when you're writing your website or blog that you emphasize what you are offering over and above the competition. Connect the offering to the benefit, so 'Open until late' is a statement of fact; 'Open until late for your convenience' is the element of value we want customers to engage with.

Classic marketing and sales theory is a great way of understanding customers. This is the starting point to building relevance into our messages, and if we can hit the right people at the right time with the right tweet, this can be converted into throughput and profit.

In short

- Begin with establishing your segment, then consider their lifestyle.
- Relevance is the key to great messaging: think about what your customers are doing all the time.
- The cornerstones of marketing give us insight into what customers value; use these as a starting point for great messages.
- Understanding motivation to buy helps us deliver messages that sell.

Tip

Building value means valuing yourself, your output and your contribution. Don't sell yourself short.

Section Four
The nuts and bolts of better writing: 'how to' guides on writing and editing

- gathering content;
- developing the message;
- how to write better copy;
- how to edit existing copy.

In the last section we focussed on gaining an understanding of who our potential customers are and what makes them tick. That is important stuff to know if we are going to get our messages to really hit home, but even more vital is the way we compose our outbound communication.

This is where the nitty-gritty content development information comes in. Here is a section covering ways of gathering in data, information, news and even gossip which may provide us with a useful body of knowledge which we can develop our ideas from.

When we have amassed enough ideas, how do we write them up into really punchy copy? There is guidance here for that as well as a practical section where you can try out your skills of editing. Creative writing is hard work, so there are times when we should rightly rely on content which we have developed earlier, find ways of shortening it for digital media and re-version it in a way which makes it impactful.

Chapter Eleven
Gathering content

The idea of developing really incisive content is central to effective messaging. It may even be the essential business skill of the future as our lives get busier and our thirst for relevant information greater. But where do we start?

In Chapter 9 on segmentation we examined the process of gathering customer information, so we should be starting to find out what makes them tick. From here we need to deliver against their stated and unarticulated needs. Clearly, the first part of this is the easiest, but with thought, analysis and common sense we may come to second-guess what they don't yet know they are looking for.

This chapter throws light on a process which involves understanding what our audience craves, seeking out sources of interesting content, collecting as much data and information as we can, processing it and developing a series of content development strands. These will be used to populate our messages with the kind of information which really hits home with our prospects.

Getting to grips with the audience

The hard thinking that we have done when investigating our segmentation will begin to come into its own now. Don't be intimidated into believing that a huge research budget will be needed to get under the skin of your audience; the skill here is an ability to observe, critically analyse, conclude and test our theories.

Put simply, we have to look for more opportunities to get to know our prospects.

Exercise 11.1 Observational links

Let us say your business is the sale of vegetarian and whole foods. Although we cannot generalize the wants and desires of an entire section of society based on their dietary preferences, it is fair to suggest that a significant proportion of this audience takes its social responsibility seriously. It is very possible that many of them will subscribe to a green agenda.

Search online for events they might attend and go along yourself; this might be some kind of rally or festival. Now you are in a position to observe the tastes and behaviours of your prospects. What music do they listen to, how do they dress, what income group do they fall into, what issues do they pursue, which publications do they read?

Using this information you can begin to search for sources of, for example, folk music reviews, alternative and vintage clothing stores, and politically sympathetic media. Without being heavy-handed, you can begin to reflect some of these issues in the messages you develop, making you more in tune with potential buyers.

Listening skills

On a face-to-face basis we can pick up all kinds of information, but the very media we ourselves are using for outbound messages is just as useful to us in collecting rich data. Follow customers and prospects on Twitter and soon they will begin to reveal what they are looking for; the same goes for their blogs and other social networks. The great advantage here is that we can collect this information in real time and respond with instant 'solutions'.

Be curious

Devote some online search time to finding more sources and detail on the topics which are relevant to your audience. Think of yourself as their trusted portal for many lifestyle issues and add to what is being said, both with opinion and, where appropriate, sales messages which are in line with your blogs and tweets.

Opinion and comment is important in giving our posts that stand-out quality, but opinion based on what? We need to take information and sources on board first before we can formulate our view and develop our take on the topic; inputs need to come before outputs.

The paradox is that we too are suffering from the very problem we seek to overcome, that of information overload. If part of the rationale for making messages sticky is to cut through all the noise caused by sheer volume of communication, then we need to begin by filtering our intake. Along the way, we will learn important lessons about how others create stickiness.

Put yourself in the place of your audience: what is it that they would want to know? Try to draw up a list of questions you might be asked if you came face to face with one of your readers, and use these to inform your research.

It's important to implement some strategies for taking the information on board too. If we are unable to do so quickly then all our time will be taken up with gathering and not enough on outputting.

The mistake many of us make is that we fail to self-audit. In not being brutal about our information needs, the temptation is to try and take everything in. Focus on what is important to you and make a written list of topics to find out about.

Researching sources

Try to track down the innovators in your industry and get an insight into future trends. This is often an element of stickiness as we are naturally curious to know what the next 'big thing' is.

Draw up a list of the movers and shakers, the people who have already garnered a sizeable following, those whose Twitter presence is significant or who turn up at the top of internet searches. Delve a little deeper too, to see if you can spot the up-and-comers, but balance the time you spend here as there will inevitably be a lot of pointless babble being peddled.

Don't rely on any single delivery channel to give you all you need. Clearly your greatest friend will be the internet, but try not to ignore more traditional sources, such as print and broadcast media. You could even do some research at the local library.

Keeping up to date means treating your source list as a dynamic document. Add new 'contributors' as you come across them and be ruthless when assessing the insight and stickiness of those who you'd originally considered worth following. This is how to maintain relevance.

Suck up as much of this information as you can, filter and sort it, file away the items you can use in the longer term and use the current articles and opinions to form your immediate output.

Assimilating information

The ruthlessness you have applied to your source list is also going to be a key ingredient of the next part of the process, that of assimilating the information. Too often we fail to get the kernel of an article quickly enough and this is a consequence of 'consuming' it in a reactive way. Our attitude may be, 'Let's see what this has to tell me', instead of taking a proactive approach and setting our own agenda. We can shift our mindset before we begin to read, and say to ourselves, 'What do I want to get out of this article?'

There is no doubt that research takes time, but if we could find a way of making more of that time it follows that we would be able to gather more information. Speed reading is a recognized way of doing this. Here are seven top tips on how to increase your reading speed.

Speed reading

1. Make conscious decisions about what you are going to read, don't get sidetracked.
2. Try to skim and scan. When we are first taught to read we look at each word individually. Run your eyes roughly down the centre of a page and attempt to let your peripheral vision take in the sense of the words to the left and right.

3 After skimming, accept or reject. Once you get used to quickly assimilating the main ideas in a document, make the decision there and then if you have learned enough or if it seemed on first glance to be worth delving deeper into. If it is the latter, run through it again, if not, put it on the 'finished' pile.

4 Practise makes perfect. Like lots of new skills it takes time to build your competence. At first, don't try to speed read everything. Instead set some time aside each day for this activity and your ability will build over time.

5 Set a time limit. Try at first to speed read for maybe 15 minutes only. As you get better you can increase this time period.

6 Don't go back. We often waste time when we're reading by letting our eyes skip back to the previous sentence; if we get the process right from the start there is no need to do this, saving precious time.

7 Take notes. To consolidate the information you are taking on, keep a pen and pad handy and make bullet point notes each time you finish a page or section of the text.

Processing content

Once you have gathered together a body of information it is time to begin developing your ideas and turning them into messages. As one of the central themes of sticky messaging is to have regular updates, it makes sense at the start to plan out, at least in draft form, your first couple of months of activity. Failing to do this will inevitably leave you up against a deadline, or even worse disrupting the flow of your output.

If you have built up a loyal following through regular posts and then disappear for a few weeks, you may end up undoing all the good work.

Try to bring some light and shade to this process, so map out a variety of delivery methods from straight text-based articles through to top tips, quizzes, interactive forums, statistics, results and onward links to content which complement your own ideas.

Exercise 11.2 Content strand ideas

Refer back to earlier in this chapter when we looked at the example of the vegetarian and whole food business. What content strands would you think about developing? Here are a few suggestions: read through, then consider your own strands – what might they be?

- What to pack for a festival – this could offer advice on practical things to take including some healthy snacks for the journey or 'grazing' between listening to the bands.
- Sponsor a rhino – contribute to the welfare of this endangered species, all orders placed before the end of the month have 5 per cent of their profits donated to this good cause.
- Live music review – first tweet received about the new album from folk band the OnMessagers receives free veggie hamper. This type of promotion can be repeated time and again with different content.
- Energy boosters – talk about days when our concentration or energy levels flag, what could wholefoods do to give us a lift?

Some information is time-sensitive – in fact it is up-to-date relevance which often draws people to you – but there are other items which can be fed into the system as and when you need them. Keep some of these 'in the bank' for when you don't have anything current or are pressed for time.

Allow enough flexibility in your planning to add in items which evolve or occur during the period and be aware of the fact that these may bump other content to a later date.

It will also help your readers if there is some kind of developing story or theme, so you may begin with 'An introduction to...', follow this up with 'Top tips for better...', move on to 'Advanced tips for heightened...', remembering to build in opportunities to occasionally summarize what you have said so far, which will keep late adopters on board with what you are saying.

Keep fresh

The ultimate magic word in advertising is 'new'. Although brands are built on consistency, even they need refreshing now and then, so don't get drawn into serving the same old stuff all the while. Make part of your plan to find an interesting perspective and do this with fresh sources. New players are coming on stream all the time and we can tap into their tweets, views and opinions so that we are always refreshing our own content and keeping our output energetic and dynamic.

In short

- Find out what your audience wants before developing content.
- Be conscious of information overload and make decisions about what you want to consume.
- Draw up a planned list of information sources, monitor them regularly and use their output to spark your ideas.
- Assimilate information and develop short, medium and long-term content strands.

Tip

Use metaphor and analogy. If one thing is a bit like another, make that connection for your audience to show that you understand them better.

Chapter Twelve
Developing the message

We should now be at the point of developing messages across a number of platforms. Having worked out who our audience is, thought through the lifestyle implications of their stated needs and yet-to-be-expressed desires, and sourced a spectrum of information which is in tune with them, we next need to turn all this work into hard-hitting communication which develops our brand and ultimately increases traffic, loyalty and revenue.

In this chapter we look at the necessity to link platforms together, examine how to plan a multi-channel strategy and include tips on keeping content both current and readable. Before all this, a quick thought about the backdrop of our messaging: what is it we are trying to achieve?

Sales versus happy traffic

Commercial use of social media requires a delicate balancing act. Pushy in-your-face sales messaging is likely only to be read by those in the market to buy your goods; they will be the ones actively seeking you out. Go too far towards being an information provider, a reflector of news and opinion in order to keep people interested, and you might risk forgetting about the call to action which gets consumers to buy.

Finding the balance is often about an understanding of each major channel, which we will look at in terms of how long or short

FIGURE 9 Gathering and re-versioning content

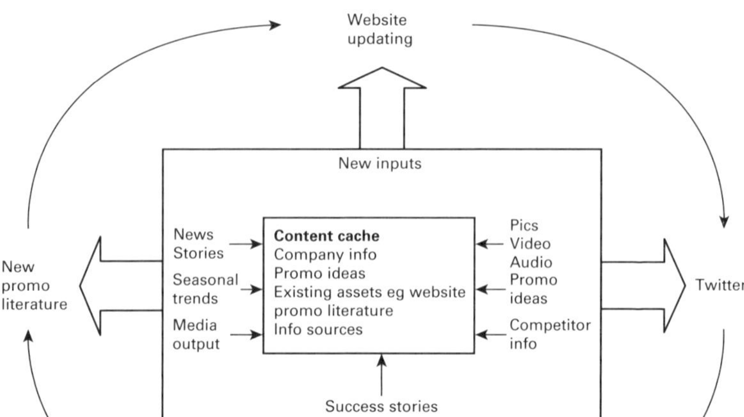

1 Centred cache contains existing info

2 Outer box lists new sources which input to the cache

3 Block arrows indicate new output

4 Outer arrows show how new content can be shared across platforms

term they are. In social media terms the longest-term outlet for our messages is our company website. Largely speaking these are set up and then left to their own devices. Occasional updates occur, but usually only when a revamp is needed. They contain the static information about the company's aims and objectives, the products or services it provides, ways of buying and contact details.

Although some larger companies set up RSS feeds so that interested parties can subscribe to their latest news, in general terms the most dynamic part of many sites is the channel we will define as medium term, which is the blog. Of course it doesn't need to be embedded in a site, it can stand alone too.

Good blogs tell stories, provoke discussion and offer opinion in a concise format which avoids rambling or digression; they get on with it, but allow the writer time to develop a theme.

The instantaneous end of the spectrum for immediate messaging and response is where a lot of the promotional action takes place. Facebook and Twitter sit here and if used properly should be directing traffic to our more developed areas of content listed earlier.

Integrated communications

What many regard as the great limitation of short-term channels can be turned to our advantage if we understand the best ways of using them. Short messaging, limited by attention spans or the number of characters which can be used, do not have to lose impact as a result. Instead we can direct readers of a tweet or Facebook post to a fuller story on a blog or website. In order to do this we may need to offer an incentive. This might mean that we need to make the longer content more desirable by offering an inbuilt reward, so promotions, giveaways, discounts or video posts can all be used to drive this traffic.

Further integration can come about by creating an 'upward spiral'. Essentially this means that the more followers you have, the greater chance you stand of gathering even more. A buzz starts to be created and outsiders want to know what they're missing out on. In a street market a crowd around a stall gathers a bigger crowd, and the same principle applies here.

Driving existing loyal users from your Facebook page to your website won't be easy, but neither is it completely necessary: they are already fans. What we are trying to do is to encourage *their* friends, who are currently unaware or unconvinced of your offering, to come and visit.

We can do this by increasing the buzz via the number of 'likes' we attract. This will raise the profile of your output resulting in its appearance in the news feeds and information tabs of your loyal fans, increasing your visibility to their friends.

Becoming more likeable

There are lots of ways of increasing the number of 'likes' your business posts get:

- In the early days get friends and family to like you – don't overplay this in the long term.
- Ask people to like you. On your landing page have a bold banner saying 'like our page': it makes it more likely that people will.
- Run a competition.
- Offer exclusive content as a reward, for example access to video that can only be viewed if you like the page, or top tips or insight delivered via an ebook format.
- Give a discount to those who like a page.

Techniques of reverse promotion occur too: in all circumstances we should be looking to direct traffic from one part of our social media mix to another. The website should have links through to other channels, with a request to 'Follow us on Facebook and/or Twitter' (or whichever other platform you are using).

Increasing our outward activity can also give us opportunities to bring people back around the loop to us, so where appropriate post comments on other blogs which will arouse curiosity, 'like' related products or posts on Facebook, or re-tweet something which you know is of relevance to your followers.

Managing the platforms

Many businesses set off on the road of promotion via social media without understanding the implications. If we were to try and manage all the separate channels as individual entities we would be spending the rest of our lives feeding that machine. Instead there needs to be integration, both in a technical sense and from a content point of view.

Planning output

The speed of a communication channel is in inverse proportion to the amount of planning we can do, so with Twitter, where one of the key elements is being able to respond in real time to what is going on, there is virtually no time to consider our content in advance. The best we can do here is to have a set of parameters (which may need to be developed over time) to indicate the type and tone of our responses. So for reasons of diplomacy we may decide not to comment on political stories or pass opinion on conflicts or disasters; it's not that we don't care about these things, but it is often better if they are kept isolated from our business interests. Similarly we may give salacious news stories a wide berth but feel able to comment on movie releases, sporting victories or the weather. Finding how safe your own territory needs to be is a matter of personal choice.

Aside from the responsive side of Twitter, part of our planning may involve developing some generic content which we can use at any time. As an estate agent you will know that most of the activity happens at the weekend so could develop a series of tweets to post on a Friday evening or Saturday morning. A deli in the centre of town would more likely choose mid-morning on a weekday when office workers might be getting hungry; use logic and market knowledge here.

Top ten tweets

As part of planning your output, try to have ten top tweets which you can use at any time to keep your audience interested. Save these for when it's a slow news day and not much of relevant interest is happening for you to respond to. Here are a few examples for a hardware store.

'A stitch in time saves 9 – fix that gutter today and treat yourself with the savings'

'Spruce up that drab radiator in 15 minutes – it's cheaper than buying a new one'

'TGIF what DIY plans do you have this weekend?'

'Fix a leak, wire a plug, pave a patio – free 'how to' guides @ www.onmessagediy.com'

In a similar way you can develop multiple strands for a blog, all of which can run in parallel. Here are three ideas; think about some more for your own sector:

1 Time-bound – relating to the changing seasons, how does it affect your business, is weather important, people's mood, what they buy and how they feel, can you reflect this back and make a connection?
2 My journey – an ongoing diary-type blog, focussed on business related topics and covering the aspects of news which affect the reader.
3 Interactive – ask lots of questions and look for suggestions from readers, then respond to these in a professional businesslike way.

As our relationships become closer and more intimate, the informality of messages increases in line; we become chattier and more at ease. Although this is a healthy part of building increasing trust, it can be undone by carelessness and taking the audience for granted. There is a crossroads where risk occurs. We need to remain vigilant to ensure we avoid the danger zone of overfamiliarity.

Don't be cheeky!

In customer interactions it is a good idea to maintain a professional deference. It is customers who ultimately are paying our bills and need to be treated with respect. This doesn't stop us having warm relationships and friendly dialogue, just as long as we always remember who is boss.

Ratner

The classic story of taking customers for granted is that of Gerald Ratner whose jewellery stores were once on every high street in the UK. Thinking he was in only the company of his peers, he joked about the quality of the products on offer in his stores.

At a meeting of the Institute of Directors in 1991 he made a speech which included references to his products being 'total crap'. As if this wasn't bad enough, he went on to say that some of the earrings were 'cheaper than a prawn sandwich'.

The media instantly picked up on the story, customers were outraged and stopped shopping at Ratners. The company dropped in value by £500 million.

Knowing what to say is clearly vital when we're messaging, but choice of platform is becoming increasingly important. We need to keep abreast of how our customers are finding their information and deliver it in ways which suit them. If they're migrating from one delivery channel to another we have to make sure we have the right presence there.

That's what multi-channel strategies are all about.

In short

- Develop a multi-channel strategy from the start.
- Crosspromote from one platform to another to maximize integration.
- Balance being an entertainer with the necessity to sell.
- Work hard at being 'liked': it will pay dividends.
- Treat customers with respect, no matter how you communicate with them.

Tip

Make 'em laugh. Using humour in messaging is very powerful; it gathers followers as long as it's funny!

Chapter Thirteen
How to write better copy

What do you think makes a great writer? Someone with a mastery of the language, a gift for storytelling, wit and insight, an amazing vocabulary and classical education. In some cases all this is true, but when it comes to writing for modern media the skill set is much more about common sense.

The kind of writing we're involved with requires an ability to get along with people, sufficient language skills to outline our ideas clearly and quickly, the odd good idea and the confidence to say, 'I've done my best, so here it is'.

Never let yourself be intimidated by other people when it comes to your writing. It is purely and simply an expression of who we are and if there are some who don't like it, that's because we can't expect to get along with everyone in life – we never claimed to be Shakespeare! The reason for saying this at the start is because the greatest inhibitor to well-written copy is self-confidence, so be bold, follow some basic rules and you will become the best writer you can be.

In this chapter we will be considering what these rules are and attempting to find ways of combining them, in order to make our written words stand out over and above others who are competing for the attention of our audience. We'll start by getting the technical issues of grammar, punctuation and spelling out of the way, then look at a stepped process to go through which will help guide our thoughts into snappy written output.

Finally there is some sound advice on style and technique.

Revision (grammar and all that)

Language changes and evolves all the time so it is sometimes hard to keep up with what is acceptable and what isn't. The acid test for new-media writing has to be, does it sound right? Stop worrying about the detail of grammar, get the basics in order, follow down-to-earth guidance on punctuation and let the sound of the copy dictate your style.

The quick guide to punctuation

- Read it aloud to find where the pauses should be. Text is almost impossible to understand if it is not broken up properly. Our natural pattern of speech will tell us where the breaks should occur: if you faint for want of taking a breath you probably need more punctuation.
- Befriend the full stop and be mean with your commas. Still, the natural tendency for many is to break up huge passages of text with lots of commas, dashes, semi-colons or ellipses... Cut down on these and use full stops instead. This keeps your thought process tight and makes the copy much easier to read.
- Not everything you write is funny! Nor is it a huge revelation! So don't feel the need to continually exclaim! Exclamation marks are a bit like swear words: the less you use them the more power they have when you do. Just as using upper case makes it look as if you're SHOUTING, so overuse of the exclamation mark makes it appear that you think you are much wittier than you are.
- Apostrophes aren't as tricky as they seem. If you want the full story, Google 'when to use an apostrophe'. The most important usage in writing for social media is where the apostrophe replaces other letters, so 'will not' becomes 'won't', 'cannot' becomes 'can't', and so on. If we are writing as we speak it is much more likely we will use the versions with the apostrophes in.
- Take a tour of the keyboard and look at all the symbols. Although @ and # have come into their own there are many which we use only occasionally. Stick with the basics mentioned above and most of the time you won't go far wrong.

Use spell checker

When it comes to spelling there is really no excuse any more for getting it wrong as the computer will do all the hard work, if we only ask it to. You will no doubt have noticed that for all its knowledge your laptop will still only point out the words which don't exist, so take the time to read back what you have written.

Spell check will be fine if you type 'the cat sat on the mat', but it will equally give the green light if you put 'the catch sat on the mat'. There is a strong argument which says we should not even be thinking of pressing the tweet button until we have re-read our work at least once.

Let's write

So, armed with these basics we are ready to begin writing.

As promised here is a seven-step guide to get your writing started. Set some time aside and make sure there is nothing around to distract you, then get stuck in and see how much fresh content you can come up with in half an hour.

Step 1: Ask, what is this about?

Before you start bashing away at the keyboard make sure you have a purpose in mind. Is this promotional copy for a new line you are introducing, or part of an ongoing blog about fashion, which suggests the need to accessorize an outfit with items from your online store? Without a sense of purpose the copy will simply wander and the reader is left wondering what you were on about.

Step 2: The one-person brainstorm

Take a sheet of paper and write down all the words and ideas which are relevant to your article, even in the most obscure way. This exercise helps us find links with other items of interest and expands our thinking in a way which may provide a new take on an old subject.

FIGURE 10 Writing triangles

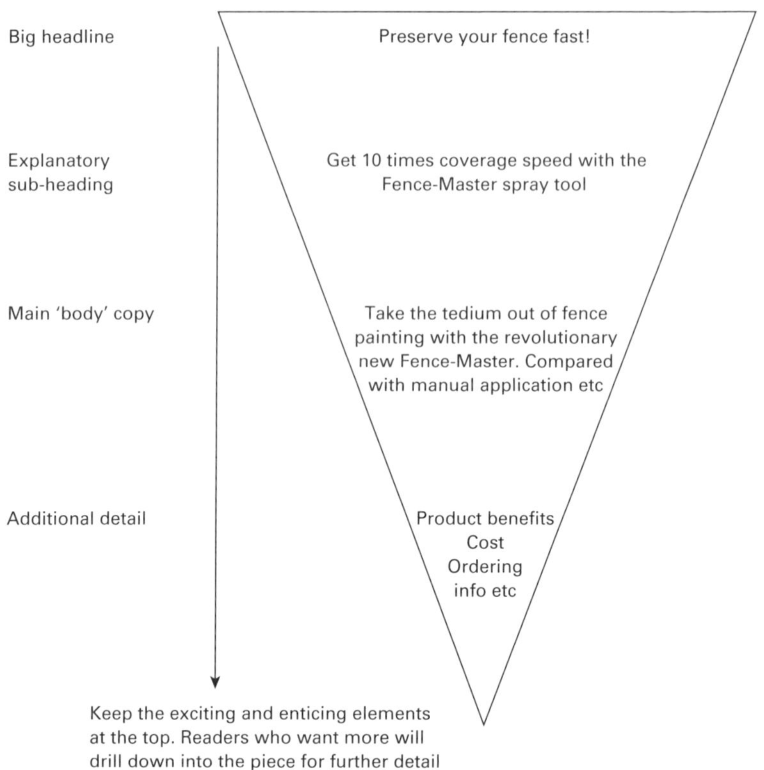

Step 3: Write like you speak

With your subject matter in mind, have an internalized conversation or monologue with yourself. This is not as crazy as it appears because by doing this you have the opportunity to imagine how a reader will 'hear your voice'. Thinking about explaining your story to a friend makes it much easier than being stifled by the idea that you have to write some award-winning prose.

Step 4: Stay within your limits

Be the best version of you that you can, but don't attempt to become like another writer you admire. A well-crafted, basic, down-to-earth piece which gives your take on the week's events (and the relationship to your product offering) is much better than an attempt to mimic the serious news output of a leading journalist. Just be you.

Step 5: Use 'short, fat, upside down triangles'

This used to be referred to as the 'inverted pyramid' style of writing, where the main story would be at the top of the article and you would have to drill down into the long tail of the upside-down pyramid to get to the detail. Now it's more important to keep those triangles short, with detail available elsewhere, by hyperlink if necessary. Only give them the headlines.

Step 6: Shock tactics are more dynamic

We might not be able to sustain the wow factor in everything we write, but it's a good aspiration to have at the start. What are we saying which is new, shocking, dynamic or exciting? Keep it snappy and you'll stand a better chance. We'd all rather read an item which was billed as 'Five ways to impress your partner' over and above one which was trailed by 'An examination of the constructs of human relationships'.

Step 7: Be active

Write in a modern, engaging 'now' style. For example, it's more exciting to say 'the man wrestled the crocodile to the floor' than 'the crocodile was wrestled to the floor by the man'.

Looking back – a review process

When you have gathered a body of work together, either existing output or new material you have just written, take time out to review it. The notes below will help you gauge how effective your copy is. If you can find a 'copy buddy' this will help too. Someone who understands your business and what you are trying to achieve with your communication can act as a sounding board and let you know the messages which really hit home.

Getting to the point

We need our messages to convey what we want with the minimum of fuss. A good exercise which helps when composing a newsletter or company blog entry is to write it first of all in bullet point form. This cuts to the chase of what we intend to say. If more detail needs to be added in order to make better sense, or better English needs to be used, it helps to have tackled the problem this way round, rather than start with pages of waffle which need to be distilled down into an understandable form.

We should keep asking ourselves the question, 'What's the point?' – both at the start of the writing exercise and when we read it back. There should be no doubt over what you are trying to convey.

The need for plain language cannot go unnoticed here. If the sign of a good education (and by association a clever person) is how well they write, it is not the quantity or floweriness of prose which will score points, but how easy it is to digest. If people confuse this use of elaborate phrasing with intelligence, you might remind them that wisdom is writing in a way your audience will understand.

Exercise 13.1 Flowery or plain?

Which of these do you prefer? What might the target audience think?

1 The establishment of this iconic edifice is part of the ongoing urban regeneration initiative, designed to ensure consumers attain a rich integration in their retail experience, encompassing the availability of sustenance in tandem with a plethora of purchasing opportunities.

2 The new shopping centre has cafes as well as shops.

The golden rules when it comes to plain language are therefore, 'Say what you mean' and, critically, 'Keep it short'. There is increasing evidence to show that we consume short sentences much more easily than long paragraphs and our recall of the meaning of what we have read is much deeper and more accurate.

Starting point

Many people launch off into the first paragraph without really thinking through what they want to say. Receiving marketing email from your favourite brand of footwear which is a pot pourri of different ideas and updates just confuses all of the issues; ultimately none of them really receive the attention they deserve.

Think hard; ask yourself, 'What is this?'

- general information;
- sales promotion;
- entertainment (with inbuilt product benefits);
- teaser campaign (building to a pay-off down the line);
- update;
- advice and tips.

Simplicity

As well as thinking hard about what you're about to say, think who to. Consider the person you are sending this to and write your message with them in mind. Combine your own personality with a sensitivity to them and their relationship with you. In these chattier days of communication it is fine to start with something personal or topical as an ice-breaker, as long as you get into the substance of the message without too much preamble.

Sample output

Blog

The following messages would be appropriate if you sold boots, camping equipment and outdoor clothing.

> I don't know about you but I always get excited when spring time comes. Once the weather picks up I can't wait to get out in the hills and blow away those winter cobwebs. This year I'm going to banish those early-season blisters! Having the right gear helps, suitable socks, a lubricant for my feet and most of all, boots that fit.
>
> I've already started my fitness regime so I can get the most out of the day. Take a look at these exercises for a 7-minutes-a-day workout. www.onmessagefit.org

Tweet

> Hill walking this Easter? Try this one tip to avoid blisters www.onmessageboots.com

Developing themes

Twitter has taught us that single themes help to maintain relevance as topics are discussed by other users or re-tweeted with comments added. The communication evolves like a set of building blocks, each placed on top of the other. It is much better to concentrate on this simplicity and let the organic nature of the medium take the story forward rather than try to explain everything at once.

Exercise 13.2 Simplicity practise

For ease, think about a movie review as your next outgoing piece of communication: the theme is set. Now consider just three things you would like to let someone know about it who has not seen the film. This reductionist attitude to developing copy will make it much more readable and understandable. Using the three bullet points below write a 50-word article that would 'sell' the movie to someone:

- a great acting performance by the lead;
- wall-to-wall action and adventure;
- a twist at the end of the film.

Pay-off

There needs to be some sense of completion at the end of any piece you write. This does not have to be in the form of a conclusion, it might legitimately be a question, provoking the reader into thinking more deeply about what you have said. You could even employ the use of a suspenseful cliff-hanger, for example, 'I'm off to research the nation's five most tranquil hideaways. I'll post the results right here next week!' Alternatively you may use the last sentence to sum up what the message has been about.

In short

- Write in your own voice and you won't go far wrong.
- If it sounds right, it most probably is.
- Be plain and accurate. Spelling and grammar still matter.
- Simple themes and ideas stripped bare will increase your clarity.

Tip

Don't be afraid to be self-deprecating; a little humility goes a long way.

Chapter Fourteen
How to edit existing copy

Do you ever get frustrated by blog entries or articles that seem to go all around the houses before coming to the point? You find yourself thinking, 'Just get on with it!' They're the ones you are unlikely to go back to. They teach us how *not* to engage.

What often happens with businesses like this is that they take their existing promotional content and simply cut and paste the parts they think fit the new media they are migrating to.

Instead they should be looking at how to shorten all their existing written assets and then find ways of developing them in an appropriate way according to which platform they are to appear on. With the vast number of delivery channels today it is hard to keep up with developing and delivering new content. That is why so many have taken the route of re-versioning what they already have; the problem they face is that their traditional copy is simply too long.

When we précis a piece of content we try to cut it down to its shortest form while still keeping the original meaning; it is a skill many of us practised in school, but few have had the opportunity to use since. Now is the time when it can come into its own.

This chapter acts as a reminder of what précis is about as well as giving you the chance to have a practise. When you've made an attempt at the article which is printed here, take the main points of précis to heart and attempt to reduce some of your company literature down to its bare bones. What you will have as a result is a piece of writing which is much better suited to a website, blog or, if you're very good, even a tweet.

The ultimate précis

Branding specialists are world-beaters when it comes to précis. For some of the world's biggest brands we need see only a single letter or symbol and we know what it stands for. Of course it takes years of investment, advertising and promotion and relentless consistency of message, but it also teaches us that ultimate précis is achievable.

Three modern examples would be the Kellogg's letter 'K', the Nike tick or 'swoosh', and the iconic McDonald's golden arches. Maybe you can think of your own. Keep them in mind when you are trying to shorten your messages.

So if the starting point is that we need to be shorter, more precise, relevant and thoughtful with our communication, how do we go about it? In order to cut through the noise we could use a machete to slash away at everything which isn't relevant, but a more incisive effect can be produced by using a stiletto to fillet out what matters.

The process of précis

The fundamental rule of all précis is to preserve the original form, as written by the author of the piece. Our role is not to add comment or opinion but to simplify the text to its shortest form, without losing significant meaning.

Précis tools and tips

Outlined here is a three-step process, which you can use as the basis of how to précis, over time you might find your own shortcuts. There is a practise exercise to follow which you can use as a way of testing your précis skills. Alternatively you can take any piece of text which is a few pages long and apply the same process, by doing this your editing skills will improve.

Although you may be used to working on screen, it will be easier in the early stages to use hard copy. Another tip, which may sound a little old-fashioned, is to use a soft pencil for your marking up and keep an eraser to hand. These rather archaic tools do still have their place.

The three steps to précis

The first step is to get a sense of what the piece as a whole is about. This is for the purpose of context, seeing the bigger picture. Once you have a feeling for what the writer is trying to convey you will be much better placed to start making decisions on what to edit out. Don't be tempted to make margin notes or to underline certain passages at this stage instead concentrate on what was in the writer's mind.

When you have finished reading try to encapsulate the ethos of the passage in a single sentence, this is not only good practise of your précis skill, but also delivers a kind of mission statement for the piece, a core offering which you can keep at the front of your mind as you work through in more detail.

The second stage is the real beginning of the editing process. With your author's mission statement in mind, re-read the passage carefully with two objectives. Firstly, look out for the major points which are made in support of the overall purpose; and secondly, try to notice the transitions which connect one part with the next; these are the flow points of the article.

Underline words or short phrases which seem pertinent and try to avoid the temptation to highlight whole sentences. This is where good old-fashioned pencil and eraser come into their own: using a highlight pen may make the text stand out more, but on paper it cannot be undone. If summarizing words occur to you during this stage, note them in the margin.

On the basis of the first two steps you should now be ready to write a summary of the article. You have understood the overall tenet of the piece with the initial read through and on this basis have gone on to pick out the most relevant parts.

As you write your own version, try to summarize ideas and shorten arguments but, as stated earlier, avoid the temptation to add your own views or opinions. This is an exercise in encapsulating the author's intent, not a commentary upon it.

Once you have finished, check back to see if you have achieved the same core objective of the original piece. Compare your summary to the single sentence you wrote at the beginning and ask yourself if they tie up. Next, make sure you have covered the essential points the original contained and that there is a flow to the new version.

It is tempting to finish the process here, but your work will benefit if you have one last go at editing the draft you have written still further. If you have the opportunity, get a third party to read your summary. This can be very helpful in gaining an objective view of how well you've done. Firstly ask them to read your version, then the full article, so they will be engaging with the process in reverse order, as it were. Ask them if there were elements which they think you had missed.

Now, using the three-step process, create a summarized version of the article printed here. You will see a sample version of each, but try to develop your own before looking at the model answer.

Exercise 14.1 Précis

For a number of years, some of the world's most influential organizations have realized that future success means understanding what we are going to face in perhaps 2, 5, or even 10 years' time. The term 'futurology' has been coined.

This new 'science' is more complex than it might first appear. In studying it, we quickly get to understand that determining the future is about much more than relying on what has happened in the past. If you take this approach what you are actually doing is simply trend-spotting; it's easier to do, but less likely to produce startling results.

Futurology is to do with understanding the current 'state-of-the-art' and then coming to a view of how this might affect us *in practical terms* in tomorrow's world. Here are a couple of examples from a leading futurologist of things that simply wouldn't work because no one thought them through.

Firstly, a proto-type refrigerator with a computer monitor built into the door, the theory is that when first installed it is programmed to know the food you most often eat. The computer keeps an inventory of this including the 'sell-by' dates of the fridge contents (taken from barcode information) tells you when stocks are running low or dates are getting short and prompts you to buy more, or to eat up quickly. You can even link the computer-fridge to online supermarket sites so the whole job of re-ordering is done for you. This sounded like a great idea until it was pointed out that the average life expectancy of a fridge is around 12 years, whereas today's computer technology is obsolete in a matter of months; this leaves you with a perfectly serviceable fridge running an outdated operating system and software, no longer compatible with more modern versions.

Another example, again in the kitchen, is a waste bin which monitors what you throw away and in a similar way to the fridge re-orders it, taking the hassle out of shopping; it sounds marvellous, but in the real world most of us would at some point spill the baked beans down the side of the tin, meaning the bin couldn't then read the barcode and the system would fail.

According to our expert futurologist, the key to the skill is 'to have a really good think'. This means not just understanding how current technologies might link together but what the *real life practicalities* of this will be in our daily lives. The discipline also necessitates us being brutal in assessing the limiting factors (beans down the side of the tin!) if we are to have any degree of accuracy in our predictions.

The link between futurology and crisis management is that the world is now moving so quickly nobody in business can afford to stick their head in the sand and pretend nothing's happening. We have to embrace new ways of working, new attitudes and aspirations in our people and new inventions, including the all important evolution of the technology that surrounds us already. But we must do more. To be truly successful in future will necessitate us understanding how the wonders of new technological inventions can be *applied*. We must engage with the fact that 'man and machine' need to harmonize, working together in a practical not ideological sense.

In essence, to avoid crises, we all need to 'have a good think' not only about what faces us today, but the practicalities of coping with an uncertain future.

When you have written your own mission statement, compare it with the one below, then commence the process of marking up the article by underlining the relevant parts and making short margin notes.

Mission statement

Futurology is a new way of looking at what is ahead and sense-testing potential technological solutions against the practical issues which may derail them.

When you have completed your own marked up version, compare it with the one below.

Marked-up version

For a number of years, some of the world's most influential organizations have realized that future success means understanding what we are going to face in perhaps 2, 5, or even 10 years' time. The term 'futurology' has been coined.

This new 'science' is more complex than it might first appear. In studying it, we quickly get to understand that determining the future is about much more than relying on what has happened in the past. If you take this approach what you are actually doing is simply trend-spotting; it's easier to do, but less likely to produce startling results.

Futurology is to do with understanding the current 'state-of-the-art' and then coming to a view of how this might affect us *in practical terms* in tomorrow's world. Here are a couple of examples from a leading futurologist of things that simply wouldn't work because no one thought them through.

Firstly, a proto-type refrigerator with a computer monitor built into the door, the theory is that when first installed it is programmed to know the food you most often eat. The computer keeps an inventory of this including the 'sell-by' dates of the fridge contents (taken from barcode information) tells you when stocks are running low or dates are getting short and prompts you to buy more, or to eat up quickly. You can even link the computer-fridge to online supermarket sites so the whole job of re-ordering is done for you. This sounded like a great idea until it was pointed out that the average life expectancy of a fridge is around 12 years, whereas today's computer technology is obsolete in a matter of months; this leaves you with a perfectly serviceable fridge running an outdated operating system and software, no longer compatible with more modern versions.

Another example, again in the kitchen, is a waste bin which monitors what you throw away and in a similar way to the fridge re-orders it, taking the hassle out of shopping; it sounds marvellous, but in the real world most of us would at some point spill the baked beans down the side of the tin, meaning the bin couldn't then read the barcode and the system would fail.

According to our expert futurologist, the key to the skill is 'to have a really good think'. This means not just understanding how current technologies might link together but what the *real life practicalities* of this will be in our daily lives. The discipline also necessitates us being brutal in assessing the limiting factors (beans down the side of the tin!) if we are to have any degree of accuracy in our predictions.

The link between futurology and crisis management is that the world is now moving so quickly nobody in business can afford to stick their head in the sand and pretend nothing's happening. We have to embrace new ways of working, new attitudes and aspirations in our people and new inventions, including the all important evolution of the technology that surrounds us already. But we must do more. To be truly successful in future will necessitate us understanding how the wonders of new technological inventions can be *applied*. We must engage with the fact that 'man and machine' need to harmonize, working together in a practical not ideological sense.

In essence, to avoid crises, we all need to 'have a good think' not only about what faces us today, but the practicalities of coping with an uncertain future.

Finally, from your own marked-up version, write a summary of the original article and once again compare it with the version here.

Draft précis

Some large organizations are using a new 'science' called futurology which adds a practical slant to possible future scenarios as an additional sense test.

Examples of failing to account for practicalities include a combined computer/fridge where the IT becomes obsolete before the appliance, or a barcode-activated bin which monitors refuse disposal and re-orders consumables. The latter is useless if the barcode is obscured by spillages.

Futurology necessitates thinking through implications and consequences and can be used effectively for crisis-avoidance.

Compare and contrast your own version with this and note any significant differences. As mentioned above, you can get better at précis the more you practise. Try it out with a magazine article or the front page of the newspaper. When it starts to become easier take your organization's entire existing written material and apply your new skills. Brochures, media articles and even the existing company website can all benefit from this process, re-versioning your content and making it more appealing because of its brevity.

Websites with clear layouts, intuitive navigation and efficient functionality score highly over their competitors. Blogs which cut to the chase, giving readers the information and opinion they want to hear without them being bogged down in detail, are likely to gain more followers; tweets which hit the sweet spot get re-tweeted. The key element is the ability to present an offering to us which we can assimilate in a short space of time; that is where précis comes into its own.

In short

- Précis is a powerful tool for writers. It cuts waffle and saves your readers time.
- Always maintain the sense of the original article.
- Practise writing a short summarizing sentence which conveys what you have read.
- Your précis skills will improve with practise.
- Apply the rules of précis to all your existing output.

Tip

Become a serial editor, not just of inputs but outputs too. Most things are better when they're shorter.

Section Five
Advanced technique: going global, expanding creativity, storytelling and more

- expanding creative horizons;
- storytelling;
- the future.

Practise will make us all better writers. As long as we keep listening to our prospects and customers, taking time out to review our progress and honing our copy to be in tune with their lifestyle, we will continue to get better and better.

Beyond this there are some final tools and techniques to consider if we are to expand the business beyond the current horizon. International markets are available to many more businesses today than ever before, but we need to tread with caution with our messaging to gain acceptance and minimize the risk of causing offence by mistake.

Onwards and upwards, we also look at advanced methods of thinking about our messaging including the development of our creative side and the benefits and techniques for developing the skill of storytelling, an age-old form of communication that is paradoxically making a big comeback in the world of social media.

Chapter Fifteen
Crossing boundaries and going global

Time was when you opened your shop on the high street, people turned up and bought your wares, and everyone was happy with the arrangement. Things have moved on since then and now everyone has the potential to be an international player.

It is also true that for a while the only people who could expand their business beyond insular boundaries were those who had sufficient capital to set up a branch abroad. For many years that took very deep pockets as it was necessary not only to cater for the tastes of the locals, but to understand their culture too.

Case study – Unilever

In the late 1970s the UK-based foods division of Unilever tried to develop instant hummus for Middle East markets. A bit like packet soup, the powder was mixed with water to make a quick and easy version of this staple food of the region. Part of the marketing rationale is that Middle Eastern women spent many hours making fresh hummus every single day, boiling the chick peas, mashing them and adding tahini and olive oil, but now there was an alternative.

Setting aside the difficulties of replicating the real thing from a packet, what they failed to understand was that culturally these women had no problem with the existing process: neither they nor their families were looking for a 'convenience' solution. Which shows that if you don't understand all the motivations of your audience, you will fail. Culture is a large part of this.

The seismic shift in the business landscape has been based upon the enabling force of technology which we have acknowledged elsewhere. As well as giving us all the communication channels necessary to get to market, we can at the same time portray ourselves as much bigger players than we really are. Working out of an office in the spare bedroom at home is no barrier to creating a professional-looking online presence which has the appearance of a much larger enterprise. These days, we are all global players, or at least could be if we chose.

In this chapter we look at the impact this has on how we communicate. How can we successfully cross boundaries, not so much from a language barrier point of view (in fact this is easily solvable in most cases today) as from a cultural and values viewpoint?

As well as looking at the differences we might encounter in other markets, we shall also examine how using fundamental business principles allied to simple, plain language will take us a long way into the heart of a new market, giving us acceptance and building rapport with an entirely new customer base.

This is of direct relevance to businesses which are trying to exploit the whole market, irrespective of geography; but if you are not in this category there is still a lot to be learned here. Although you might not be reaching out to 'link hands across the water', this does not mean your existing customers will be inclined to always continue to shop local. You may not be global, but they are!

Finding similarity and celebrating difference

Engaging with people in new markets can happen as a consequence of finding things we have in common, but also by understanding and being interested in the differences between us. This is not just to do with tastes, but culture and behaviours too, as often this will drive how we integrate with each other, define the boundaries of acceptability and influence the method and tone of our communication. In polite cultures like the Far East it pays to be polite. This may come across as stand-offish in a gregarious South American context. Follow the lead of the host country and you won't go far wrong.

We should be aware when communicating in a multicultural environment there is potential for confusion. There are some basic steps we can all follow when we're crossing boundaries which will minimize the risk of misinterpretation.

Researching your new markets

For a small business the thought of market research can all be a bit scary; apart from anything else, it sounds expensive. When Mars or McDonald's conduct research the costs are proportional to their size and what they want to find out. As a smaller organization our research needs are more generalized and the need for pinpoint accuracy is lessened. All we are really trying to ascertain is whether there is demand for our output, what the price point is, how the competition operates and, most importantly, how to deliver our messages in terms of both channel and content.

The first thing to say is, 'Don't panic!' You don't need all this information at once; it is okay to build it up over time. However, the rule is to tread carefully at first until you have amassed some market knowledge.

Here are some suggestions on how you can research a new international market.

Online

This is obvious. There is a lot of intelligence that you can gather without leaving your desk. An internet search will turn up all kinds of market reports, anecdotes and opinion for free. This is called secondary data, it has been collected by someone else, and as long as you use a broad range of it rather than pinning all your expectations on single source, it should yield good results.

As well as seeking out market reports which will tell you the potential of the territory, try to get a sense of what it is like to do business. Most of all have a good look around the online presence of potential competitors. It may even be worthwhile purchasing a small amount from them, to get a feel for how transactions take place.

In person

If possible and affordable, visit the place and see for yourself. Wandering aimlessly around will be of little benefit, so try to arrange as many appointments as possible with potential customers or even competitors. You might even consider some kind of partnership arrangement, where each of you represents the other in the respective territory. Informal discussions are fine at this point, but if a contract is to be drawn up, use a qualified legal representative.

Develop a network

Part of our communication strategy is about getting others to follow us through sticky messaging. By doing this we can begin to foster two-way communication, asking for feedback and input. Here is an opportunity to get some incisive knowledge from people who know. Ask opinions about who is best in the market, what they like about existing purchases and where their unsatisfied needs are. You may need to set up a competition, incentive or promotion to encourage response, but the knowledge you gain will be worth it. A good rule of thumb when entering a new market is to keep asking questions until an understanding of the new challenges is gained.

Trusted friend

The idea of having a presence in the new country is an excellent one; it can provide real-time feedback on what is happening. The responsiveness you are able to display at home just because you have your finger on the pulse can now be extended abroad.

How do you find such a source? It makes sense to nurture an existing relationship rather than seek out a new one, so a loyal customer would be a good place to start, someone who you are already trading with. You can make a customized approach, outline your requirements for market information, ask if they will vet your outbound communication and offer some reciprocal reward, like a level of discount, so that both parties benefit.

Guidance for cross-border communication

The most important advice when communicating across boundaries is to stay in safe territory at the start. Just as when we form personal relationships, this is facilitated by sharing small, non-threatening morsels of information with each other, gradually building in intimacy as both parties get more comfortable, so the same lesson applies to our entry into new territory.

Irrespective of which national tongue is used, there are some basic rules which will keep us safe and as a consequence increase the power of our written messages. These can be applied to good effect at home, but are even more important than ever when an overseas audience is the target.

Plain

Great scholars or erudite orators can sometimes lapse into using a form of language which is almost impenetrable. This has no place in our international business messaging; after all, we are seeking to persuade rather than show how clever we are.

All that floweriness is often a way of disguising the fact that you don't really know what you're talking about, so people will be much more impressed by clearly articulated strong ideas, put simply. When a new audience is trying to assimilate complex information, let them use the majority of their brainpower on the issue in hand, rather than trying to unravel the language you have dressed it up in.

Always be as explicit as possible and avoid the use of your own colloquialisms and idioms; these are sophisticated language tools for the lifetime linguistics scholar, not the casual trader.

Short

Irrelevant drivel is one of the worst time-stealers. Keep it short, make it say what you want and then finish.

Placing this kind of rigorous demand on how we say what we say puts the onus on us to get to the heart of the message. Inside our heads we may be taking complex ideas, then sorting and sifting them into more manageable concepts. The very process of this helps in our analysis, making it easier to make sense of the issue.

Exercise 15.1 Practise brevity

Write a 150-word review of the last restaurant experience you had, for example:

> The room was large and spacious, although it had preserved a degree of intimacy through clever use of lighting. At the door we were greeted politely and shown to our table. Olives and other nibbles were quick to arrive as we pored over a mouth-watering menu, etc, etc.

Now turn this into five bullet points, for example:

- 'an excellent restaurant with an intimate feel';
- 'service is swift, polite and responsive'; etc.

Exercise 15.2 Brief and to the point

Repeat the above exercise with a description of the nature of your business. Think of what you would say in prose then summarize it in bullet form for an international audience, remember the rules of simplicity and plain language.

Incisive

Stripping messages down like this gives us the chance to make them more pithy and easier to assimilate. By taking time at our end, we save the receiver time at theirs, which in itself contributes to the effectiveness of the messaging. The more we practise honing our messages, the better we become.

Exercise 15.3 What are we messaging about?

Use the five steps below to develop a simple international proposition. With each bullet point there is a practical example to illustrate how the content should be populated.

1. Product or service – define what this is, for example an online shop selling materials for making greeting cards.
2. Feature into benefit – what is the consumer getting? For example a wide range of accessories, fact sheets and 'how to' guides to start making cards right away.
3. Gratification – what is the immediate reward? For example the simple satisfaction of the hobby allied to making friends and family feel valued by receiving a hand-made card.
4. Long term – is there any lasting benefit? For example a newly acquired skill which can be used again and again.
5. Repeat purchase – where is the future business opportunity? For example new products, styles and fashions in cards, the continuation of the hobby or the start of a bespoke card-making business.

Unambiguous

We need to fight harder than ever if we are to prevent ambiguity creeping in when we're talking to different nations or cultures.

Developing standardization

The move towards global branding has taken over 50 years and a number of products have changed their name in order to fall into line. In the UK, 'Oil of Ulay' changed to 'Olay', to match its Continental equivalent; similarly 'Jif' became 'Cif'.

Prior to this, manufacturers simply attempted to sell the home-branded product abroad and on one notable occasion a soap brand name turned out to be the Spanish word for part of the male anatomy! It pays to sort out this ambiguity from the start.

As an aside, Kodak were thought to have chosen their iconic brand name because it meant nothing in any language.

Illustrated

There is no substitute for great copy when it comes to messaging; you have to get the words right if you are going to prick the psyche of an audience. However, the world is a multi-media place and because of increases in bandwidth the former luxury of being able to squirt rich content around is now taken for granted.

Consider using pictures, illustrations and graphics and video to enhance your messages, particularly in global markets, as a way of overcoming language barriers. Think how safety information on flights is now often conveyed via a seat-back screen using little in the way of words and much more animation to illustrate the procedures. Pictures can be a really powerful tool in cutting through language barriers.

It is easier than ever to expand our businesses into the global market and the perils can be ameliorated by sound common sense. Be polite at all times, ask lots of questions, deliver on promises and keep on learning. Stickiness principles will apply just as well at home or abroad and this is an essential element of building audience, followed by sales revenues.

In short

- Our world is becoming smaller; we can appeal to wider markets.
- We can celebrate both similarity and difference. Each teaches us lessons about better communication.
- Shorter words and simpler phrasing allow less leeway for misinterpretation.
- Say what you mean, cut the waffle, and your ideas will be better articulated.
- Supplement your words with pictures. Illustrate the points you make.

Tip

Nothing was ever lost by being polite; it's a great place to start any relationship.

Chapter Sixteen
Expanding creative horizons

Uniqueness is paradoxically our universally shared trait. No matter how many people populate the planet no two will ever be exactly the same, and it is this individuality which quite literally sets us apart from everyone else.

The highly energizing part of this is the realization that our idiosyncratic voice can be developed in a way which will never be copied and, if managed correctly, will be highly 'readable'.

The process of this development would quite naturally sit within the domain we call 'creativity'. The more we can expand on this, the greater potential impact of our messages. So this is a chapter which puts creativity under the microscope and attempts to make sense of it. Although finding a suitable definition might be hard, there is no reason why we cannot learn more about being creative through the process of our thinking. In order to develop this aspect of our writing and communication there are also a range of exercises to stimulate your thoughts and get you into your own creative zone.

There are creative geniuses in every field who we may stand back and admire. Sometimes we can be overwhelmed or awestruck by their inventiveness or artistic skill or ability to problem-solve. Indeed part of the point of creativity is that it cuts across so many areas of our lives. But aside from Einstein, Picasso, Brunel or more latterly Steve Jobs there is an opportunity for all of us to exercise more creativity and inject it into our writing.

If we think of creativity as ideas, inspiration or revelation our conventional view of the true creative genius is they have what have become known as 'light bulb moments'. These are the flashes of pure genius which solve a problem or invent something entirely new, or alternatively spawn artistic creations which are aesthetically inspiring.

But if such ideas are predicated on the mystical lighting of the bulb, from who knows where, we may as well give up trying. The truth of creativity is that it does rely on a spark of inspiration at times, but such sparks only really begin to fly when we work at making them do so.

James Dyson provides us with a brilliant example of this. Although he is credited with revolutionizing the design of the vacuum cleaner, this wasn't done via a single spark of genius. Instead he built many many prototypes in his garage before even getting near to the iconic cyclonic invention which now graces so many homes.

So, it is better to think of creativity as a muscle which we can exercise to develop our idea-generating ability and find inspiration more easily. Once applied to our messaging, we should soon have others recognizing our uniqueness and strength of ideas. But how do we go about this? Here are three simple exercises.

Exercise 16.1 Eskimos and snow

We've all heard that Eskimos have many more words for snow than the rest of us, so sometimes our creativity needs to be stretched by context. As much of what we offer our customers is in answer to some need or other, take 10 minutes to write down all the words you can which relate to 'solution'. Use some of these when you're next blogging about an offer.

Exercise 16.2 Child's play

Much of what we're trying to communicate needs to be reduced to its simplest form so take the leading story from one of today's 'serious' newspapers and rewrite it for a seven-year-old.

The trick here is to use plain language without being patronizing; you'd be amazed at how savvy the average seven-year-old is these days!

In future when you are writing new pages for your website apply this 'seven-year-old' rule.

Exercise 16.3 Lifestyle linking

Think of any model of car, picture it in your mind's eye: the colour, age and physical appearance. What is the lifestyle of the driver? Write down which brand of breakfast cereal they eat, what shoes they wear, which films they like, their values.

Don't fret over whether you are right or wrong, it's your ability to test your imagination to get a full picture of customers which is important. Keep your own version of customer lifestyle in mind when you are writing.

Creative writing – developing a workable strategy

When we sit down to write in a creative way, two things happen. Alongside the 'creative' words we write comes a creative thinking process. This can help with problem-solving as we are often able to see the world in a different way. It may be the key to unlocking a puzzle.

The process of creative writing is an excellent starting point for developing this aspect of ourselves. Instead of waiting until we are put with a group to brainstorm, be proactive and regularly set time aside for creative writing. In this way we can add a useful discipline to our portfolio of skills.

The benefits of this exercise can be twofold: firstly, we might come up with ideas which solve some of our own business issues; and secondly, the very act of regularly writing in this way improves our communication skills – it's about exercising that creative 'muscle'.

Despite other time pressures, it is best if you can set aside a period each day when you get the chance to practise this kind of writing. It doesn't have to be for long, but the regularity is useful, as over time we get into the swing of creative writing. Also, don't be inhibited by worrying over content: by its nature creative writing is an exercise which often begins with no agenda.

Seeing the creativity of others in action can also be highly energizing, it can bring about a positive competitiveness in work, leading to better and better ideas being forwarded. If you can arrange a session of creative hot-housing with others, you may all go away from it with many more ideas than you'd expect.

So, if you have pledged to improve your writing skills the first thing to do is to remove the block. All of us have heard of this legendary obstacle called 'writer's block' which prevents us from expressing ourselves in the way we would like. This 'problem' needs to be reframed to get us generating ideas again. There may be plenty of occasions when you feel you are not writing to the best of your ability, but there is never a time when you cannot write. If you're struggling for ideas you won't find any by inaction, only by taking positive steps.

Getting started

There is a Dutch expression which sums up the inertia that lots of professional writers feel. Roughly translated it says, 'I have a no'. This means if we never ask we will not know whether the answer would be positive or negative. The state of 'no' is what we currently possess. If we're looking for a 'yes' we have to take action, we have to do something, we have to ask the question.

If you worry over whether you will be creative or not, a consequence is that you don't try to be. Then it is guaranteed that your prophesy will come true. Only by forcing ourselves to attempt some

FIGURE 11 MindMapping® technique

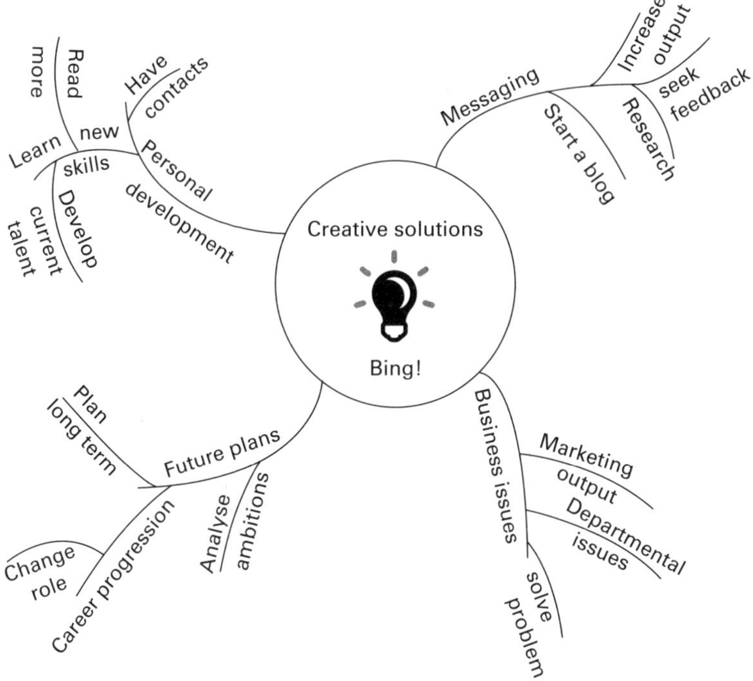

idea generation will we find out if we are able. So it is vital to discipline yourself to set aside 'creative time'.

Next it is good to strike a balance between your free-thinking side and your logical, more disciplined inclinations. A way of corralling your thoughts to focus on some interrelated themes is to map them out in a pictorial way, in a spider diagram or mind map.

> The recognized expert in mind mapping is Tony Buzan. The process begins with a central theme, often expressed in the form of a diagram or graphic. From here main branches are drawn to show the big ideas that you might want to examine, and each of these leads to individual areas of interest. When you have completed the outline, like the one shown, you can add thickness to the lines which are most important or colour code your map.
>
> Often by 'seeing' all the elements at once we get a better idea of how to prioritize our activities.

Also, keep an 'issues sheet' nearby where you can record any other extraneous thoughts which might prompt further writing in future. This means you are sufficiently free and creative to allow your consciousness to wander into new territory but have a system in place where you can 'park' such thoughts to save you being distracted. It may be as part of your planning you save a session a week for revisiting this sheet and attempting to develop your more unusual ideas a little further.

Mix things up

Think of your writing like a training session: you're trying to build 'stamina' and 'strength' so that your ideas don't come as occasional one-offs but in a constant stream and they each contain sufficient 'power' to make them worth using. If you think of your creative training in this same way it will avoid boredom and help to keep you energized.

Exercise 16.4 Stretching your creativity

Here are a few ideas to stimulate your thoughts:

- Devise a new mission statement for your company or strap line for a product you sell, based on absolute candid honesty.
- Compile a list of bullet points that typify a great blog. With each one, write a sentence of additional explanation.
- Reply to a fictitious letter of complaint, setting the record straight from your organization's point of view.
- Pretend you run your own multi-million-pound company. Write a 50-word email to staff to rally them.

Cut yourself some slack

Ideas and creativity come on a sliding scale from brilliance right down to mediocrity. There are very few people who can be at the top end every day, so don't be concerned if you don't hit the mark every time.

What is more important is to prove to yourself that you have the rigor and discipline to keep working at this craft. It is this 'perspiration' which will prove beneficial in the long run, and if you look back over your writing you will see discernable improvements.

Getting into a panic about not coming up with anything creative is much more likely to frustrate and inhibit you. In time this will, not surprisingly, begin to lead downwards into a spiral of non-creativity.

Find the right time

Our bodies operate on a daily biorhythm; it's what we think of as our body clock. This affects our alertness, propensity to exercise, concentration and many other things. It has an impact on how creative we might feel at any one time. Maybe for you it would be pointless to wait until late in the day when tiredness may make you less likely to come up with ideas for sparkling tweets or blog content. Alternatively you may be the kind of person who likes to feel you have cleared the decks of whatever else has to be done in order to free your mind to roam unencumbered. There are some for whom the early morning period, just between sleep and wakefulness, can be a highly creative time.

It is worth experimenting to find out when you are at your most creative; you may be surprised by the results, and once you discover what is most effective you can fit your creative time around whatever else is in your schedule.

Record your spontaneous thoughts

Quite often miniature light bulb moments occur when we least expect them and as a consequence they can easily be lost. Some people report that they can wake in the night with a creative idea, perhaps as the result of a dream (Mary Shelley claimed she dreamt *Frankenstein*). If this is the case it will almost inevitably be lost if you fall back to sleep without recording it. Many creative people keep pen and pad at the bedside and capture these thoughts for further analysis in the cold light of day. In the same way, you can keep a journal or diary near at hand and note down significant revelations as they occur.

Review your efforts

A human failing is to always be looking ahead to what is not yet done, rather than sometimes pausing to see how far we have already travelled. On the plus side, this attitude can fuel our career ambition so that each time we ascend another rung of the ladder we are energized to keep pushing for the next.

However, if we are not careful, it can equally result in dissatisfaction: we are never really happy with where we are. Make sure this does not happen to your creative efforts by making time to sit down and review the journey so far.

The three-step review process

This is a quick, easy way of measuring your creativity over time. It requires some reflective time and is reasonably subjective, but no less valid for all that.

1 Define your version of creativity (perhaps its 'writing great tweets', or 'sporadic wit in my blog'. Don't overcomplicate this; it is simply how you would outline to a third party your ambition to drive more creativity into your writing.

2 Think about measures and timescales. Weekly or monthly is a legitimate frequency for review, longer than this and you'll probably forget what you've done. Weigh up the volume of your output and give yourself a percentage mark for how creative overall you have been. Pick out a single piece of writing as your best work.

3 Over time, compare the results with the previous period to assess what you are doing better and what needs more work; it may be that your output increases but your percentage suffers. Think of remedial measures if necessary, or if things are going well consider what it will take to move up to another level. Build up a library of best work and review this periodically. Think about what circumstances drove you to write these and try to replicate them in future.

Specifically, we are concerned with communication and how to add impact to our messages. A higher degree of creative thinking is an essential element of this, but it also has many spin-offs in the workplace.

Over time both the substance and the style of your messages will improve. You will be able to better get to the nub of a problem, and have a more intuitive understanding of what others want and expect. You can then match your method of delivery in terms of the style you choose, to make a real impact.

Understanding the barriers to creativity

We've probably all got to the point where we believe the technology at our disposal far outstrips our usage of it. Whatever the device, it can do all sorts of things we don't even know about. This is a good metaphor for our creativity. The truth is that it is probably boundless if only we took the time to use it more, learn about it, discuss it with others and experiment. So what is stopping us? Creativity is in the main free of charge, it can make us feel great, help solve problems, make other people laugh – what prevents us using it all the time?

When we look at the common barriers none of them is insurmountable, but it will take conscious effort and occasionally courage on our part to overcome them.

Time

A manager was overheard to say, 'I don't have time for staff appraisals, I'm too busy managing them'. The point is that the process of appraisal is the same as management, it's just work in progress. So when we get stressed about not having the time to be creative it is because we are seeing it as some process separate to the rest of our lives. Of course it is good to set time aside for creative thinking and writing, but mostly we can marble it through the rest of our activities; it's simply a process of training ourselves to 'think creative'.

Additionally our fixation with 'task' in our lives will always mean there is 'stuff to do', so if you wanted to excuse yourself from any creativity, ever, it would be easy. The truth is that creativity adds value, it makes something new which wasn't there before, whether that's a fabulous sculpture or a tantalizing tweet. What could be more energizing? Under those circumstances the lawn can stay unmown for another day.

Letting go

Particularly when it comes to writing, most of us have a fear of what we'll call 'letting go'. So you have composed your blog, re-read it, checked it for mistakes, gone through the process of précis and you're ready to publish. That's when misgivings begin to creep in. The insecurity we all suffer about whether anyone will like what we've written can be stifling.

We talk extensively about 'finding our voice' and sometimes we just have to use that voice and take a leap of faith. If others don't like it at least we can say that it is authentic and a fair reflection of us, rather than a watered down 'try-not-to-offend-crowd-pleaser'.

It's easy to look back at what we wrote 10 years ago and cringe, but we do the same when we look at what we wore back then; in both cases it was probably just 'of its time'. Sometimes it turns out to have been surprisingly good and we're faced with the challenge of recapturing that freshness.

Take a deep breath and publish, what's the worst that can happen?

Fear of failure (or success)

If we're trying to put creativity into our writing and it simply doesn't flow we might begin to believe it's a skill which is beyond us. This will become a self-fulfilling prophesy if we let it. Not writing is a surefire way of not being a success.

By the same token, if we've had a spell where everything we touch turns to golden prose, we may begin to feel intimidated by our own success. What happens to the musician who has a fantastic first album? Usually they struggle with their second 'difficult' album. It is ludicrous to assume our early success can't be repeated: after all, the ideas came from us in the first place so we have proven the case for our creativity.

Keep these barriers in mind and use them as a context for developing creativity.

Don't ever get drawn into believing you are not creative. Just because someone else can draw or sculpt or cook better than we can it doesn't mean they have the creative gene and we don't. We are all capable of coming up with ideas and implementing them in a unique way. At first this can be quite exposing and that is where the risk lies: others may not like what we do. However it is a risk worth taking as it allows us to contribute in a major way to our unique voice. More than anything, this is what an audience is looking for.

In short

- Our value is in our uniqueness, creativity is a way of helping us to express this.
- Sometimes the 'light bulb' will illuminate of its own accord. It is much more likely to happen if we put in the groundwork.

- Setting yourself a 'creative writing agenda' adds rigor and discipline to your idea generation.
- Allow time and space for your creativity. Variety is more likely to preserve your interest.
- Practise seeing the world with other people's eyes; you will become much better at responding to an audience in a relevant way.

Tip

'New' is the golden word of advertising; try something new to give your creativity a boost.

Chapter Seventeen Storytelling

There is a danger as our messages get shorter that we may miss the point of them altogether; even worse, that our audience might do the same. This is why stories are a great way of keeping cohesion in what we are saying. When we write we need to sometimes remind our readers of the point of our story: what is it saying about the wider picture we are trying to portray about our business?

Stories have other great benefits too; they help people really relate to what we're saying much better than any set of facts and figures. Furthermore, stories well told are memorable, portable and potentially viral. This means that learning is embedded deeper for longer and at any point in the future may get retold to a fresh audience, spreading our word further afield.

So this chapter will take a look at storytelling, charting its roots, significance and key elements, so we can better understand how to collect, enhance, retell and create stories. These techniques can be used to turn our messages from fact-givers into entertainment, increasing their stickiness along the way.

The first storytellers

In the days before pen and ink much of society's learning came in the form of stories, anecdotes and parables passed on from one to another, often through the generations, from father to son, mother to daughter, tribal elders to followers. When we examine how this happened, it is often interesting to note that these stories rarely remained static, they evolved over time according to both the whim of the storyteller and the number of people the story had passed through. You will already be familiar with the concept of 'Chinese whispers', a phenomenon which happens in many families where the truth is bent over time for comic effect or in order to airbrush the past! With business stories the same often happens, where we refuse to let the truth get in the way of a good story. As long as we are doing this for the purposes of entertainment, rather than defamation, we will be on safe ground!

Why stories work

We have an enduring fascination with each other as people. This is what supports much of the media. Our inquisitiveness over what happens in the lives of others drives sales. Stories are often classified as 'human interest'. With or without television, radio, newspapers or online, such stories have always fascinated. Gossip over the garden wall was the same thing, but transmitted usually one to one, instead of one to many (hence the word 'broadcast' implying the larger audience). Think about the things you would like to know and it will drive you towards richer content for your audience; our curiosity is likely to be their curiosity. Good starting points are things like the human element, news which is truly new, behind the scenes, insights into behaviour and intelligent comment. Here is just one example:

Exercise 17.1 The next big thing

Being 'ahead of the curve' gives you a great advantage when blogging about your business. You don't even need to have invented or developed the 'next big thing' but simply to know about it before other people.

Whatever business you are in, start to research sources of up-to-date knowledge which you can use to feed your messaging pipeline with. If you have the opportunity to network with people from your industry sector, geographical area or business type this can be a great way of tapping into knowledge and keeping up to date.

Where our best stories come from

To gather together a great collection of stories is easy, but it can be time-consuming. This is based on the premise that 'stories are life'. Things happen to us on a daily basis which can form the starting point of a story. Also, we are frequently told stories by friends and colleagues, perhaps about something in the news, how difficult their journey to work was or the row they had with a family member at the weekend. Sifting what is relevant is the difficult part, but by making a conscious effort to do so we have the ability to build up a bank of stories that can be used in different circumstances.

Where possible try to see linkages between the different elements of life so that you can employ analogy in your stories. Likening a slow tortuous journey to work to the way decisions are taken in large corporations will ring bells with many people.

Making stories effective

We don't have to take all stories at face value. If we're trying to make a point it is legitimate to enhance and retell a story in a form which makes it easier to understand, more digestible or even funny. Bending stories to fit with the point we're making is fine, as long as we're not presenting them as factual. One of the difficulties of many stories is that they contain too much unnecessary detail which clogs them up and gets in the way of the moral or punchline. Try where possible to cut out anything which is not adding to the story. When you have written your story, re-read it and critically appraise it with emphasis on its brevity.

Although when we're blogging or tweeting we don't want to be seen to use the same story over and over again, it is equally true that stories usually benefit from being 'worked'. We often find this when retelling a joke; it gets funnier the more we hone it. The same can be done with stories if we adapt them across different platforms, but avoid too much repetition where possible.

Whether you collect your own stories, adapt what you hear on a day-to-day basis or use online research methods to find new sources there are always ways of improving your raw material. In order to do this it is helpful to understand what makes a great story and this is outlined below.

Seven inputs for better stories

1. Emotion in storytelling

One of the great benefits of stories is that they often appeal on an emotional as well as logical level. We assimilate the facts of what we're hearing but the much more powerful part of the story is the set of feelings it engenders in us.

In practical terms this means that if we are to become a trusted source for those we are messaging, it is much more likely to come about because our story has an emotional pull, rather than being yet one more summary of statistical data.

Thinking about human interest is a good starting point to understanding where the emotion in a story lies. Where anger and frustration abide we have the chance to offer a solution (with our product or service); alternatively if we all love lazy Sunday afternoons a luxury armchair from our new furniture range may complete the experience. It is all about making the connection from emotion to solution, without being too contrived.

2. Fact finding for stories

The whole landscape of research and knowledge has changed with the advent of the internet. Prior to this time, if you wanted to garner even widely held data you had to farm the company database or visit the local library to get a relevant book on the subject. Now, with the use of a search engine we can find out just about everything on just about anything. The instant availability of all this information can bring our stories to life, add credibility and increase interest.

Sometimes it's good to let the internet take you where it wants to, so begin by setting up a search and then follow links from one site to another, browse in the old-fashioned way and you'll be surprised what you will turn up. When you inevitably hit upon a site of real quirkiness and interest be sure to save it in your favourites and by building a collection of interesting sources you will always have a pool to dip into for your stories.

3. Character

Perhaps the most compelling part of any story is the person in it. We may not be able to recreate the great characters from fiction, but there are modern traits which our audience can relate to. What picture do you conjure up when you hear the word 'geek' or 'boffin' or 'siren'? You will have met your own characters and can use traits of them to create new ones to bring your stories to life. Think about what your ideal hero would be like, or consider how you would typify someone thoroughly dislikeable; this is the starting point to great character creation.

Exercise 17.2 Messaging through character creation

Make up a figure who is central to your message and paradoxically it will add reality to it for your audience. Here is an example; after reading it, try to think of your own:

> A survey of staff reveals that the worst bosses are the ones who never say thank you, take their employees for granted and are self-centred. It's even worse if they have bad breath!
>
> The antidote is to reward yourself with a selection from The Chocolate House, order online at www.onmessagechocs.co.uk

____

____

____

____

____

____

Sometimes we illustrate a point (like the necessity for resilience) by using a third-party character.

> At 83 years of age Mrs Blumenthal was still not the kind of woman to let the system defeat her. An ex-hospital matron, she was used to organizing people and coping with adversity.

A classic case of using a character to bring a story to life was during the US presidential campaign in 2008 when Republican John McCain continually referred to 'Joe the Plumber' as a metaphor for middle-class America. The real origins of 'Joe' are a matter of dispute, but some sources claim he was an ordinary citizen who had taken Democrat (and later President) Barack Obama to task over his tax policy on small businesses.

Simply attacking policies would have taken McCain only so far, but giving a personality to the story made it real for many more people. In their mind's eye they could visualize Joe and make a connection with him; if they related to him they could believe in him as their representative, challenging policies they thought flawed.

4. Plot

Stories are like a journey we take the reader on; a passage from A to Z with stop-off points along the way. Even a long-running drama serial has subplots between different characters. The real skill is to interweave these with the main story so they don't become a distraction.

With any plot there is good reason to have a logical flow of events, a sequence that builds. This not only adds interest to the tale, but also helps to embed the learning which underpins the story. Many leading advertisers have used this technique to build audience loyalty and interest, Renault's 'va-va-voom' campaign is an example, alongside 'the Oxo family' and a series for Nescafé Gold Blend coffee which featured a burgeoning romance.

With each episode (and this applies equally well to a blog) our audience can be sustained by the use of suspense, a feeling that we want to know what happens next.

5. *Curiosity*

We were taught at school that stories should have a beginning, a middle and an end, and while this basic structure holds true, it's a good idea to refrain from always filling every detail: often readers like to do that for themselves. Sometimes it is more interesting if we are asked to use our imaginations to complete the story.

Author J.K. Rowling had unparalleled success with her series of seven Harry Potter books and later claimed that the entire story had come to her fully formed. Eeking out the twists and turns of plot kept readers interested throughout the long process of telling the tale.

When you are recounting your personal or business story, what is the timeline? Which events are most important? How did things evolve to where they are now? Going forward, what will drive your development or growth? Map this story from the start and you can begin to chart each 'episode' in a blog.

6. *Resolve*

Contrary to this, a self-contained story is like a completed message, it is 'resolved' at the end. We get to find out who committed the murder or won the race.

This is worth remembering when we are sending outgoing messages. A blog may contain anecdotes of events, but the bigger picture is the ongoing tale of our lives.

Within our tale there may be running themes, each of which we can build separately with a sense of 'watch this space' to keep the reader engaged. A combination of resolved stories and ongoing threads makes for a good balance of messaging.

You might outline the origins, principles and values of your business in a series of blog posts, a sort of 'how we got here' piece. This can be complemented by current news about what is happening with expansion, ideas in development, products to be launched or new personnel in the organization.

7. Punchline

Some stories not only 'resolve' but they also have some kind of powerful ending, perhaps intended to shock the reader or surprise them in some way. Often it is this unexpected element which keeps audiences engaged until the end, just to see what happens. The classic version of this is the joke, but not all punchlines have to be funny, they can be reflective or quizzical as well.

Some of the best endings involve a twist in the plot, a moment when we might say, 'I didn't see that coming'. Far from being disappointed in these endings we are often energized at having been challenged. When so many outcomes in life are predictable, a bit of variety is welcomed.

Snickers twist the plot

An early inventive use of Twitter for advertising and sponsorship purposes came via the chocolate bar Snickers.

A series of uncharacteristic tweets from celebrities Rio Ferdinand (a Premiership footballer) and Katie Price (a British glamour model and reality TV star) were resolved with a message about the confectionery.

Footballer Ferdinand surprised fans when he claimed to have taken up knitting, while Price, more famous for her glamour than her insight, tweeted, 'Large scale quantitative easing in 2012 could distort liquidity of govt. bond market.#justsayin.'

After a quick-fire series of messages, each celebrity tweeted 'You're not you when you're hungry @snickersUk #hungry #spon'.

This is great use of a punchline which packs a powerful message.

Understanding and employing these elements of storytelling can really bring our messages to life. So when you have worked out your message in terms of what you want to say, think about it in

FIGURE 12 Group storytelling exercise

Step 1
Form two groups of three

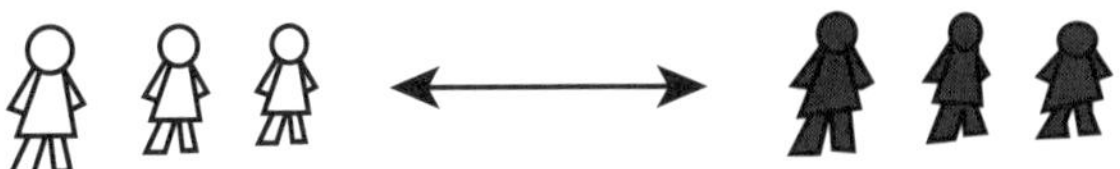

Step 2
Each team member tells a short, personal story to their own group

Step 3

Each group selects one story. Team members make up a version personalized to themselves

Step 4

Whole group re-forms. The stories are re-told in their various versions. The opposing team has to identify who is telling the truth

terms of a story. Employing the elements of a great narrative can turn a dull sales message into something engaging and energetic, it can make your audience sit up and take notice.

If you get an opportunity to develop storytelling in a group environment, the exercise on the previous page is useful in stimulating creativity, it's also great fun!

In short

- Storytelling is an age old way of passing on messages and making them memorable.
- It is fine to collect stories and adapt them, or we can invent our own.
- Good stories contain emotion and should promote a similar feeling.
- Take the facts and try to add a narrative: it creates and sustains interest.

Tip

Be surprising: everyone loves a surprise.

Chapter Eighteen
Revision, consolidation and the way forward

The big players in business will always dominate any competitive landscape but what has changed forever and for the good in recent times is the opportunity afforded to all of us to establish, develop and sustain a business of our own. Beyond the core principles of deciding what you want to sell and to whom, the great enabler of commercial success is communication.

We have observed that the number of channels is opening up more and more each day and how connectivity with audiences gets both stronger and increasingly available. At the same time there is a merging of communication methods and the old elite are having to make way. We can all be journalists now: personal branding and public relation (PR) are part of everyday commercial life, and marketing communications of the most precise and targeted kind are within our reach.

In this final chapter, we have an opportunity to review some of the key messages of the book so that we can consolidate our thinking on the topics which have been covered. By the same token, it's good to take a look forward and think about how these newly acquired skills can be used to full advantage. What can we do from here to keep on improving; where are the sources of future learning and how will we apply the new thinking in a business context?

Change

Everything we do in business is different; each communication we despatch has a new significance. The audience is ever changing in its makeup and attitude and we have to keep pace. Channels of delivery are constantly evolving and we need to track progress and stay on board. The most significant of all the changes is the nature of the way we work and interact, which is faster, more demanding and higher pressured than ever before. We no longer have the luxury of, or the appetite for, reams of prosaic prose. We need to get to the point. Now.

In future, don't think about how you can stay 'on message' by developing content and then turning it sticky, instead try to train yourself to 'think sticky'. Look at every communication opportunity in terms of the impact the right message could have. The famous and the feted get re-tweeted as a matter of course, the rest of us have to fight it out with the competition. The best way of doing this is to work on being different, finding a unique voice and tweeting with 'significance', not just the first thing that comes into your head.

The power of sticky messages is not just what they say (although that is important too), but also what they are. Get this right and you are providing a service to your audience, imparting information in an easy-to-digest way. The more skilled we become, the easier their lives will be in 'consuming' what we send.

Behind the scenes

There used to be two faces to every business, the one it showed its customers and the one the staff saw. Now, everything is open to inspection so take control of this with your own business and go hunting to find out about others.

Offer your customers insight into what goes on to drive your business forward. You don't have to share the cash flow projections with them, but photos, video and personal stories from behind the scenes are always of interest. This is especially beneficial if you are able to show that you live the values of the company all the time. If you proclaim to be socially responsible and some of that comes through in the way you recycle or choose suppliers, this will all reinforce your proposition and sustain credibility.

Use this 'access all areas' pass to uncover the secrets of other people's success. Online you can seek out case studies and tips for successful communication. An obvious route for greater insight and help is to search for 'ways to use Twitter successfully' or similar searches. All the major channels now provide services for small business users, offering 'how to' guides, tips and up-to-date thinking on optimizing usage. There are no longer any secrets about effective exploitation of the communication platforms, but you may need to go looking for the answers if you are going to stay current.

Solutions are already at hand so that we can manage our messaging across multiple platforms, and this search for optimum integration will continue, so we can ensure that our output will be delivered in the most appropriate way to our audience, at exactly the right time.

It is also highly likely that a degree of consolidation will take place, with stronger players becoming dominant as uptake of their platform reaches critical mass. This in itself will become a barrier to new market entrants, but the landscape is so fast-moving that not even today's market leaders can afford to be complacent. The upshot of this intense competition from a user point of view is we can look forward to ever-richer services with added-value features which will facilitate even better communication. Keep in touch to make sure you don't back the wrong horse in the future. If you pick up that a new channel is making waves, get in there quickly and have a look around; you want to be sure to be an early adopter if you are going to stay ahead.

Once the audience begins to migrate from one platform to another, because of either technological development or trend, you need to know where they are going to turn up next or you may end up shouting loudly in an empty arena.

Be active and reflective

Social media is a part of everyday life now, it's not something new and special but rather the way we communicate today. Don't be intimidated by the pace of change; now is not the time to panic.

Irrespective of what happens to alter the landscape there are some principles of communication which will always remain. Knowing who you're talking to, planning a campaign and delivering with consistency will continue to stand you in good stead.

Resist the tendency to get drawn into the maelstrom and always play your own game. Make time to keep up with what is happening, but also to reflect on the success your communication is having. Learn from this and carry on doing the activities which add value to your customers and your business.

Trends

If you want to know where the media trends are, look in the media. It sounds obvious but to make it work we need to think about what is behind a trend. Who would have thought ten years ago that cookery would become a mainstream television genre? Look behind the success and you find that the style of programming has evolved. Long ago it moved from instruction to personality. We stopped watching what was being cooked and looked at who was cooking it.

Think hard about how these steps in evolution can happen and you will equip yourself to trend spot.

Media trends tell you about messaging, but keep a watchful eye on the evolution of your own business sector: who is doing what and, more importantly, why are they doing it?

Five points to remember

As far as revision of what we have learned is concerned there are five final points which are worth considering as you prepare yourself for your communication-rich future, things which balance all the newness with some strong founding principles.

You are in control

With so much going on in the communications landscape it is easy to feel as if it's all slipping away from us. It sometimes feels as if a massive leap forward happens every day, with the introduction of a new piece of hardware or a surge in popularity for the latest digital trend.

You can take control of this process, in the same way as you oversee all other aspects of your business. Daily you manage risk, implement processes, develop strategies and 'deliver' to customers; communication is not so different from the rest of this planned activity.

Big players still dominate the landscape, so track what the Googles, Facebooks and Twitters are doing. Of course keep a watchful eye out for new kids on the block, but let the big boys act as your mentors. Their brand value must count for something.

Some things never change

Just because there has been an explosion in communication – not just in what is available, but also in how we do it – this does not detract from the fact that some principles of business remain unaltered and will continue to do so.

Great businesses are built on doing the right thing, consistently and with competence. The transactions which occur benefit both parties and each should come away satisfied with the experience.

These guiding principles should underpin our communication strategy where we need to act with integrity and propriety to establish ourselves as credible players in our market. In the rush for greater messaging, don't ignore what has always made your business tick.

Think sticky – be sticky

You don't need a degree in marketing to know that repeat business is much preferable to seeking out new contacts all the while. With our messaging now we need more than ever for our audience to keep on liking us. Every outgoing tweet or blog should be designed to reinforce our standing in the market. Deliver consistently with insight, information, wit and something fresh and new to keep customers engaged. Make them stick.

Save your loyalty for customers

No matter how well you are getting along with the channels you currently use for communicating with customers, don't get wedded to them. Next week something new might come along so treat your current relationship as one of convenience. Reserve your feelings of loyalty to the people who ultimately pay the bills, the customers. Keep serving them via the channels they choose to engage with and it is more likely that they will reciprocate your affection.

Keep getting better

Standing still will soon result in falling behind. When everything is moving on at such a pace, we need to make sure we are in the slipstream, always close to the leader. Continuous improvement takes monitoring, thought, effort and ambition, but these are the traits which are the stock-in-trade of successful businesses. The fact that they can now be applied to communications makes no difference. Set some ambitious targets and use the new skills you have developed to help achieve them.

Crossover

One way of expanding into untapped audiences is to understand the principles of crossover. The music industry has been doing this for years, getting artistes from different spheres to duet together so that a country and western audience becomes exposed to rock and vice versa.

This comes down to what we said earlier about understanding your target group: what else is in their lives, how can we piggy-back that preference? If you retail fine wines, link your messaging, content and promotion to fine food. Offer discount vouchers to a top restaurant in your area or free recipe tips.

Beyond this, are your audience opera lovers, prestige car owners, festival-goers? The more you can discover about them the better your messages will become.

Be yourself

The business world is hyper-competitive, the blogosphere is clogged, billions of tweets and texts are sent every year, so how in the middle of all this can you make a difference?

Whether our audience expresses it overtly or not, the fact is that it is us they want to see or hear; that individual spark, underpinned by our personality, which sets us apart from everyone else. Were this not the case, we could get computers to generate our communication. Once you realize that it is you who is special, your set of attributes, life experience and knowledge which will impress an audience in a way which is truly idiosyncratic, you are halfway to creating really powerful, impactful communication.

That will keep you on message.

Further Reading

Bounds, A (2007) *The Jelly Effect: How to Make Your Communication Stick*, Oxford, Capstone

Buzan, T (2002) *How to Mind Map*, Wellingborough, Thorsons

Hatton, A (2007) *The Definitive Business Pitch*, Harlow, Prentice Hall (Financial Times)

Heath, D (2007) *Made to Stick: Why Some Ideas Survive and Others Die*, London, Random House

Maslen, A (2010) *The Copywriting Sourcebook: How to Write Better Copy, Faster – For Everything from Ads to Websites*, London, Marshall Cavendish

Sloane, P (2011) *A Guide to Open Innovation and Crowdsourcing: Advice from Leading Experts in the Field*, London, Kogan Page

Theobald, T and Cooper, CL (2012) *Shut up and Listen*, London, Palgrave MacMillan